FRANCIS FRITH'S

THE
CHILTERNS

PHOTOGRAPHIC MEMORIES

MARTIN ANDREW is an architectural and landscape historian and writer on outdoor matters who is the Conservation Officer for Wycombe District Council in Buckinghamshire. He specialises in the landscape of lowland England, and combines his love of history, landscape and architecture in his writing. Since 1978 he has lived in Haddenham in Buckinghamshire with his wife and children. He is a keen long-distance walker, and enjoys riding his classic motor cycle round the country lanes of the Chilterns. He was born in Doncaster, but spent most of his childhood in Ealing and Carshalton in Surrey. After university he worked for the Greater London Council's Historic Buildings Division, Buckinghamshire County Council and Salisbury District Council before joining Wycombe District Council in 1990.

FRANCIS FRITH'S
PHOTOGRAPHIC MEMORIES

THE
CHILTERNS

PHOTOGRAPHIC MEMORIES

MARTIN ANDREW

First published in paperback in the United Kingdom in 2011
ISBN 978-1-84589-557-0

Text and Design copyright The Francis Frith Collection®
Photographs copyright The Francis Frith Collection®
except where indicated.

The Frith® photographs and the Frith® logo are reproduced under licence from Heritage
Photographic Resources Ltd, the owners of the Frith® archive and trademarks. 'The
Francis Frith Collection', 'Francis Frith' and 'Frith' are registered trademarks of Heritage
Photographic Resources Ltd.

British Library Cataloguing in Publication Data

The Chilterns - Photographic Memories
Martin Andrew
ISBN 978-1-84589-557-0

The Francis Frith Collection®
Unit 6, Oakley Business Park,
Wylye Road, Dinton,
Wiltshire SP3 5EU
Tel: +44 (0) 1722 716 376
Email: info@francisfrith.co.uk
www.francisfrith.com

Printed and bound in England

Front Cover: **CHALFONT ST GILES**, *The Village c1965* C498043t
Frontispiece: **CHESHAM BOIS**, *Bois Lane c1955* C693006

*The colour-tinting is for illustrative purposes only, and is not
intended to be historically accurate*

Aerial photographs reproduced under licence from Simmons Aerofilms Limited.

Historical Ordnance Survey maps reproduced under licence from Homecheck.co.uk

Every attempt has been made to contact copyright holders of illustrative material. We will
be happy to give full acknowledgement in future editions for any items not credited. Any
information should be directed to The Francis Frith Collection.

AS WITH ANY HISTORICAL DATABASE THE FRITH ARCHIVE IS CONSTANTLY BEING CORRECTED
AND IMPROVED AND THE PUBLISHERS WOULD WELCOME INFORMATION ON OMISSIONS OR
INACCURACIES

CONTENTS

FRANCIS FRITH
VICTORIAN PIONEER

FRANCIS FRITH, founder of the world-famous photographic archive, was a complex and multi-talented man. A devout Quaker and a highly successful Victorian businessman, he was philosophical by nature and pioneering in outlook.

By 1855 he had already established a wholesale grocery business in Liverpool, and sold it for the astonishing sum of £200,000, which is the equivalent today of over £15,000,000. Now a very rich man, he was able to indulge his passion for travel. As a child he had pored over travel books written by early explorers, and his fancy and imagination had been stirred by family holidays to the sublime mountain regions of Wales and Scotland. 'What lands of spirit-stirring and enriching scenes and places!' he had written. He was to return to these scenes of grandeur in later years to 'recapture the thousands of vivid and tender memories', but with a different purpose. Now in his thirties, and captivated by the new science of photography, Frith set out on a series of pioneering journeys up the Nile and to the Near East that occupied him from 1856 until 1860.

INTRIGUE AND EXPLORATION

These far-flung journeys were packed with intrigue and adventure. In his life story, written when he was sixty-three, Frith tells of being held captive by bandits, and of fighting 'an awful midnight battle to the very point of surrender with a deadly pack of hungry, wild dogs'. Wearing flowing Arab costume, Frith arrived at Akaba by camel sixty years before Lawrence of Arabia, where he encountered 'desert princes and rival sheikhs, blazing with jewel-hilted swords'.

He was the first photographer to venture beyond the sixth cataract of the Nile. Africa was still the mysterious 'Dark Continent', and Stanley and Livingstone's historic meeting was a decade into the future. The conditions for picture taking confound belief. He laboured for hours in his wicker dark-room in the sweltering heat of the desert, while the volatile chemicals fizzed dangerously in their trays. Back in London he exhibited his photographs and was 'rapturously cheered' by members of the Royal Society. His reputation as a photographer was made overnight.

VENTURE OF A LIFE-TIME

Characteristically, Frith quickly spotted the opportunity to create a new business as a specialist publisher of photographs. He lived in an era of immense and sometimes violent

change. For the poor in the early part of Victoria's reign work was exhausting and the hours long, and people had precious little free time to enjoy themselves. Most had no transport other than a cart or gig at their disposal, and rarely travelled far beyond the boundaries of their own town or village. However, by the 1870s the railways had threaded their way across the country, and Bank Holidays and half-day Saturdays had been made obligatory by Act of Parliament. All of a sudden the working man and his family were able to enjoy days out and see a little more of the world.

With typical business acumen, Francis Frith foresaw that these new tourists would enjoy having souvenirs to commemorate their days out. In 1860 he married Mary Ann Rosling and set out on a new career: his aim was to photograph every city, town and village in Britain. For the next thirty years he travelled the country by train and by pony and trap, producing fine photographs of seaside resorts and beauty spots that were keenly bought by millions of Victorians. These prints were painstakingly pasted into family albums and pored over during the dark nights of winter, rekindling precious memories of summer excursions.

THE RISE OF FRITH & CO

Frith's studio was soon supplying retail shops all over the country. To meet the demand he gathered about him a small team of photographers,

and published the work of independent artist-photographers of the calibre of Roger Fenton and Francis Bedford. In order to gain some understanding of the scale of Frith's business one only has to look at the catalogue issued by Frith & Co in 1886: it runs to some 670 pages, listing not only many thousands of views of the British Isles but also many photographs of most European countries, and China, Japan, the USA and Canada - note the sample page shown on page 9 from the hand-written Frith & Co ledgers recording the pictures. By 1890 Frith had created the greatest specialist photographic publishing company in the world, with over 2,000 sales outlets - more than the combined number that Boots and WH Smith have today! The picture on the next page shows the Frith & Co display board at Ingleton in the Yorkshire Dales (left of window). Beautifully constructed with a mahogany frame and gilt inserts, it could display up to a dozen local scenes.

POSTCARD BONANZA

The ever-popular holiday postcard we know today took many years to develop. In 1870 the Post Office issued the first plain cards, with a pre-printed stamp on one face. In 1894 they allowed other publishers' cards to be sent through the mail with an attached adhesive halfpenny stamp. Demand grew rapidly, and in 1895 a new size of postcard was permitted called the court card, but there was little room for illustration. In 1899, a year after Frith's death, a new card measuring 5.5 x 3.5 inches became the standard format, but it was not until 1902 that the divided back came into being, so that the address and message could be on one face and a full-size illustration on the other. Frith & Co were in the vanguard of postcard development: Frith's sons Eustace and Cyril continued their father's monumental task, expanding the number of views offered to the public and recording more and more places in Britain, as the coasts and countryside were opened up to mass travel.

Francis Frith had died in 1898 at his villa in Cannes, his great project still growing. The archive he created continued in business for another seventy years. By 1970 it contained over a third of a million pictures showing 7,000 British towns and villages.

FRANCIS FRITH'S LEGACY

Frith's legacy to us today is of immense significance and value, for the magnificent archive of evocative photographs he created provides a unique record of change in the cities, towns and villages throughout Britain over a century and more. Frith and his fellow studio photographers revisited locations many times down the years to update their views, compiling for us an enthralling and colourful pageant of British life and character.

We are fortunate that Frith was dedicated to recording the minutiae of everyday life. For it is this sheer wealth of visual data, the painstaking chronicle of changes in dress, transport, street layouts, buildings, housing, engineering and landscape that captivates us so much today. His remarkable images offer us a powerful link with the past and with the lives of our ancestors.

THE VALUE OF THE ARCHIVE TODAY

Computers have now made it possible for Frith's many thousands of images to be accessed almost instantly. Frith's images are increasingly used as visual resources, by social historians, by researchers into genealogy and ancestry, by architects and town planners, and by teachers involved in local history projects.

In addition, the archive offers every one of us an opportunity to examine the places where we and our families have lived and worked down the years. Highly successful in Frith's own era, the archive is now, a century and more on, entering a new phase of popularity. Historians consider the Francis Frith Collection to be of prime national importance. It is the only archive of its kind remaining in private ownership. Francis Frith's archive is now housed in an historic timber barn in the beautiful village of Teffont in Wiltshire. Its founder would not recognize the archive office as it is today. In place of the many thousands of dusty boxes containing glass plate negatives and an all-pervading odour of photographic chemicals, there are now ranks of computer screens. He would be amazed to watch his images travelling round the world at unimaginable speeds through internet lines.

The archive's future is both bright and exciting. Francis Frith, with his unshakeable belief in making photographs available to the greatest number of people, would undoubtedly approve of what is being done today with his lifetime's work. His photographs depicting our shared past are now bringing pleasure and enlightenment to millions around the world a century and more after his death.

THE
CHILTERNS
AN INTRODUCTION

I HAVE LIVED within sight of the Chiltern Hills for twenty-five years, and worked and walked in them and written about them throughout that time. The more I get to know these chalk hills, with their intimate tree-lined valleys or golden corn-rich rolling plateau fields, their small hamlets around fine but unpretentious churches, and their superb historic market towns in the valleys, the more I love them. These hills are remarkably close to London, and very beautiful; not rugged, admittedly - you have to go further afield to find that sort of thing - but immensely popular for days out. Most car parks, such as that in Buckinghamshire's Hambleden Valley, or at Hughenden Manor, or Bedfordshire's Dunstable Downs, are packed at weekends. Many park to walk the impressively well-maintained and waymarked public footpath system; others to picnic, admire the view, stroll a few yards or visit the many attractions ranging from Whipsnade Zoo to the many country houses open to the public, such as Luton Hoo, Chenies, West Wycombe, Greys Court or Stonor Park.

The Chiltern Hills are part of the Cretaceous sedimentary rock ranges that dominate the lowlands of England. The extent of the chalk is vast, and not all as hilly as the Chilterns. It runs from Flamborough Head through the East Riding of Yorkshire and down through Lincolnshire (in both counties named the Wolds); it disappears into the Wash, and reappears as gentle hills and rolling countryside in Norfolk and Suffolk, turning westwards through north Essex. The chalk ridge becomes the Chilterns as it marches through the counties of Bedfordshire, Hertfordshire, Buckinghamshire and Oxfordshire. Crossing the River Thames in the Goring Gap, the chalk continues westward as the Berkshire, Lambourn and Marlborough Downs. In south Wiltshire and Hampshire, where a vast expanse of chalkland includes Salisbury Plain, the chalk divides and heads off eastward to form the North Downs and the South Downs, while a third arm heads off south-westwards into Dorset and the Isle of Wight. The beauty of chalk countryside has been recognised nationally by the designation of extensive areas of it as Areas of Outstanding Natural Beauty. Apart from the Chilterns, many chalkland areas have been so designated, including the Lincolnshire Wolds, the North Wessex Downs, East Hampshire, the

Sussex Downs and the Kent Downs. Many of these also have Countryside Commission Long Distance Footpaths running through them and along the chalk hills, including the North Downs Way and the South Downs Way. The Chilterns have the Ridgeway Path that crosses the Thames at Goring; it starts near Avebury in Wiltshire, and continues through the Chilterns to finish at Ivinghoe Beacon.

The Chilterns share with the South and North Downs a relative narrowness and a strong escarpment that tends to dominate the lowland vales below. Indeed, the escarpment rears up from the Vale of Aylesbury almost five hundred feet, giving emphasis to the hills and at the same time giving long views northwards from the top of the escarpment at places like Coombe Hill or Ivinghoe Beacon, and similarly at other points along the escarpment, such as Deacon Hill near Pirton, east of Luton.

The Chilterns have always been an effective barrier to expansion from London, with routes confined to the valleys and gaps. Indeed, recent archaeological work seems to suggest that the inner parts away from the river valleys were thinly settled well into the Anglo-Saxon age. Where routes heading for the Midlands and the north have cut their way through, one tends to find all forms of transport in close juxtaposition. For example, the Bulbourne valley around Berkhamsted has the Roman Akeman Street, its 18th-century turnpike successor, the Grand Junction Canal of the 1790s (now the Grand Union), the railway of the 1830s and the A41 dual carriageway by-pass of the 1990s running through it. A similar tale could be told of other routes through the Chilterns, or of other parts where valley gaps do not exist, such as the Henley to Wallingford road; this had to toil up steep hills and across the plateau before descending to Wallingford. Walking or driving around the more hilly and rural Chilterns, one is struck by the smallness of the villages, many little more than hamlets, and by their generally small-scale and simple parish churches. This was not a heavily populated region, and

HARPENDEN, *The Old Cock Inn c1965* H25066

11

some villages, such as Radnage (west of High Wycombe), do not have any recognisable village centre, just scattered farmsteads and cottages in winding, narrow-laned valleys.

The towns of the Chilterns are mostly ancient, with markets dating back to the centuries immediately after the Norman Conquest. They served large agricultural areas, and some, such as High Wycombe, became important grain trading centres. This is an ancient trade – indeed, one should not get too hung up on Chiltern beech woods as the main source of income. In Roman times the Chilterns were important contributors to the empire's corn needs. One of the Roman villas at Hambleden appears to have specialised in growing corn for export via the River Thames to feed Roman garrisons and towns in Britain. Arable fields still dominate parts of the Chilterns, particularly to the east either side of Dunstable and around Wycombe, and to the west where the hills descend towards the Thames. Mixed farming was the norm, and sheep were important in the Middle Ages for wool and later for the London mutton trade.

Dairy farming grew in the 19th century, again with an eye to supplying London's voracious appetite.

The furniture industry, particularly centred around High Wycombe, led to much former downland and arable being planted with beech, chestnut and hazel for coppicing. This made the Buckinghamshire Chilterns more wooded than before the 18th century. The dominance of the Luton straw hat industry in the eastern Chilterns increased the areas under arable to feed that industry in the 19th century. Elsewhere, many of the commons, such as those east of Berkhamsted, ceased to be grazed and reverted to woodland. The Chilterns had always been well wooded; the woods - like College Wood east of Goring - were managed from the Middle Ages for timber, coppice and woodland grazing.

The Chilterns are not high in a mountain sense - the high point in Wendover Woods is 876ft - but being chalk, they are cut into by river valleys such as the Ver, the Gade, the Misbourne and the Chess, or by dry valleys and combes. Some of these valleys have seasonal streams or

HAZLEMERE, *Inkerman Hill c1960* H470003

'winterbournes', such as the Hambleden Brook or the Hughenden Stream. Until many water extraction licences were revoked or modified in the later 1990s, the amount of water taken had effectively reduced rivers like the Gade or the Misbourne to winterbournes or non-existence. Things are better now, and even the Hughenden Stream winterbourne flows all the year round. These rivers are a delightful feature of the Chilterns; many of the towns grew up in their valley bottoms, such as Amersham, High Wycombe, Chesham, Berkhamsted and Hemel Hempstead. In the Oxfordshire Chilterns there are few if any streams, apart from those emerging from the spring line at the foot of the hills (there is one in a view of Ewelme, page 95, E59023). Up on the plateau, which is clay with flint caps, there are ponds; around them hamlets have grown up, such as Colehill, view C496010, page 65. To the south and west the boundary of the Chilterns is set by the River Thames, which flows through Wallingford and past Henley and Marlow, both important river ports until the 19th century, and then turns south beyond Little Marlow and away from the Chilterns.

Other Chiltern market towns lie at the edge of the hills where valleys cut through or routes descend, such as Watlington, Wendover, Tring and Dunstable. Many of these and other historic towns are illustrated in this collection. The 19th and 20th centuries saw considerable expansion, partly caused by the railways allowing commuting into London, and partly by localised industrial growth. Slough, High Wycombe, Hemel Hempstead and Dunstable/Luton show the greatest expansion. High Wycombe, for example, grew rapidly in the 19th century thanks to chair-

making and other industries such as paper making; indeed, there were over thirty watermills along the River Wye powering papermaking, dye works, fulling mills and corn mills. Luton, of course, had its hat industry, which was replaced in the 20th century by heavy engineering and Vauxhall cars. So development ranged from railway-based Metroland commuter housing, such as Amersham on the Hill or Harpenden, or riverside towns served by the railways, such as Goring, Henley or Marlow; self-contained suburbs grew around Luton, for instance, or (from 1947 onwards) at the New Town at Hemel Hempstead.

At one time it looked as if development would sprawl out all over the Chilterns – they are so close to London, and such a pretty and desirable area for commuters to live. However, by 1960 the Metropolitan Green Belt saved the Chilterns, and their specific special status was recognised by designating the hills an Area of Outstanding Natural Beauty in 1964. The designated area excludes all the larger towns and their suburbs, but runs from the Oxfordshire Thames boundary eastward to near Hitchin, with (which is not surprising) a gap around Luton. Thus we hope that the future of this fine and unique landscape is safe, ensured by a combination of natural features and human intervention. Natural is something of a misnomer for landscapes wherever man is found: the hedges, fields, woods, towns, villages, hamlets and farmsteads lie over the natural and give it its character, which is shaped by these human responses to the landscape and the economic needs of its inhabitants.

It is man's contribution over thousands of

years that has given the Chilterns their present appearance, and this introduction can only point out a few elements in that history that is all around the visitor. One of the most obvious links with the distant past is the Upper Icknield Way that runs along the northern edge of the Chilterns above and on the spring line. This is a Neolithic trackway and trading route from the flint mines of Norfolk to the south-west, becoming the Ridgeway once it crosses the Thames at Streatley. The Lower Icknield Way, which is parallel but lower down the slope, is thought to be a Roman route. On the hills the most obvious structures are the hill forts and causewayed camps. Some overlook the northern vales, such as Boddington Hill above Wendover or Ravensburgh Castle near Luton, or Danesfield above the River Thames; some control valleys and strongpoints within the Chilterns, such as Desborough Castle near High Wycombe or Cassivellaunus's fortress/town by Wheathampstead. Burial mounds and barrows from this distant past are also found, such

as those around Whiteleaf Hill above Princes Risborough.

The other remarkable early physical relic is the series of linear earthworks known as Grim's Ditches. These have a ditch on both sides of a central rampart or bank, and seem to be boundary markers rather than defences. Current theory is that these earthworks are Iron Age boundaries between tribal groups or estates. The Anglo-Saxons thought these sorts of things the work of gods rather than man, and called them Grim's Ditches, Grim being one of their gods. One of the best stretches of these awesome linear earthworks runs north-west from Downley above High Wycombe to Great Hampden for over six miles, while another spectacular section runs from Nuffield for four miles to the River Thames. There are other long stretches in Buckinghamshire and Hertfordshire as far east as Pitstone Hill.

The Roman period has left visible remains ranging from those of Verulamium at St Albans, which include high sections of the city wall, to

MARLOW, *High Street 1890* 23689

excavated and unexcavated villas, and above all their road network. The roads later named Watling Street (the A5) and Akeman Street (the A41) cross the Chilterns. There are other lesser Roman roads. The Romans also improved the much older Icknield Way, building a small town where it crossed Watling Street at what is now Dunstable.

The name of the hills is first recorded in Anglo-Saxon times in the Tribal Hidage, a seventh-century document, which refers to 'Ciltern saetan' or Chiltern dwellers. Were these Ancient Britons who were gradually absorbed by Anglo-Saxon colonists from the surrounding kingdoms? In any case, the name remained. When Anglo-Saxon counties were formed in the 10th century, those that grew up to serve Oxford, Buckingham, Hertford and Bedford were expanded to include contiguous sections of the Chilterns. This gave Buckinghamshire and to some extent Oxfordshire a somewhat lopsided appearance, with their county towns oddly located; in Buckinghamshire's case the county

town eventually migrated to Aylesbury to redress this imbalance.

For those readers wishing to get more historic detail and information on the long and fascinating history of the Chilterns, I recommend that you read 'The Chilterns' by Leslie Hepple and Alison Doggett, published by Phillimore in 1992 and recently reprinted. This introduction is merely intended to give you some background to a most attractive part of the country, an area whose character is I hope captured in The Francis Frith Collection views selected for this book. They are intended to give a broad balance between towns, villages and landscape, but they are, of course, dependent to a great extent on what caught the eye of generations of Frith's photographers. The text is divided into five chapters or self-contained tours moving from east to west along the Chilterns, with photographs ranging in date from the 1890s to the 1960s to give a varied portrait of these distinctive chalk hills.

HENLEY-ON-THAMES, *The Regatta 1890* 27204

15

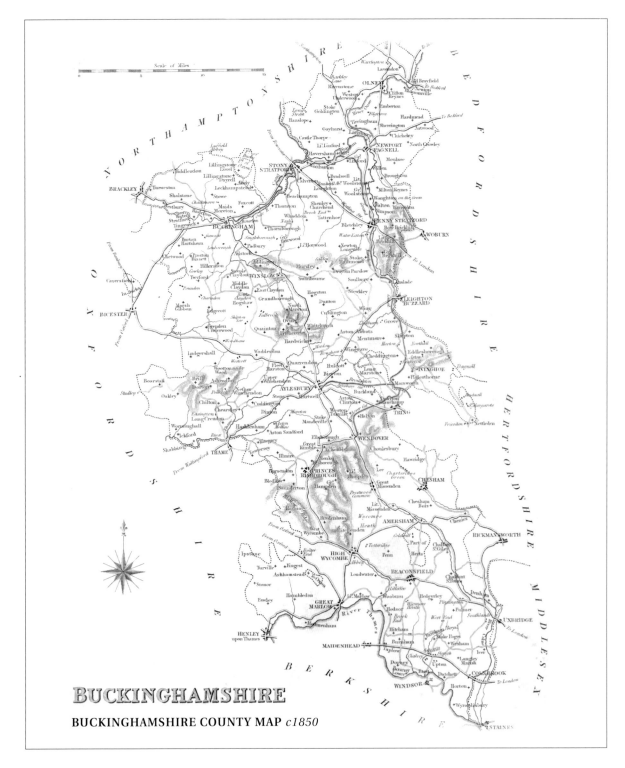

BUCKINGHAMSHIRE

BUCKINGHAMSHIRE COUNTY MAP *c1850*

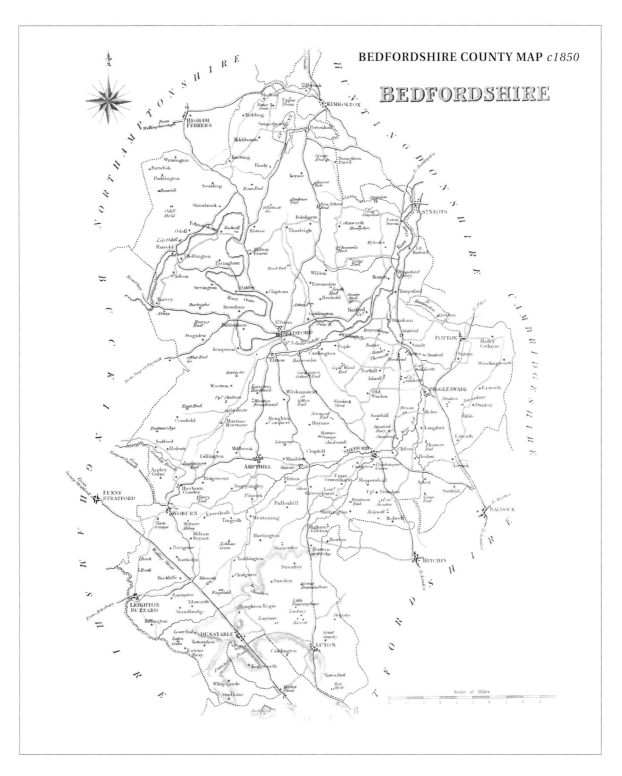

BEDFORDSHIRE COUNTY MAP *c1850*

BEDFORDSHIRE

DUNSTABLE AND THE EASTERN CHILTERNS

DUNSTABLE, *High Street 1897* 39737

Dunstable was originally a Roman settlement named Durocobrivae. With its four streets 'pointing to the four corners of the heavens', it was re-founded by the Norman King Henry I in 1119 where the ancient Roman road, Watling Street, crossed the much more ancient Icknield Way which runs along the northern foot of the Chilterns. This view was taken looking north towards that crossroads from the market place – note the horse-drawn omnibus (centre). Most of the buildings survive; those on the left infilled the north part of the market place many years ago. The old town hall tower is in the distance.

DUNSTABLE, *The Priory Church from the North-West 1897* 39743

About 1133, soon after the town was established, Henry I founded the Priory of Augustinian Canons, the nave of whose priory church survived the 1540 Dissolution of the Monasteries under Henry VIII. This had served as the parish church from 1392, and most of the monastic church and priory buildings were demolished soon after. The tower was added by the parish in the 15th century; the remains of the priory gatehouse are just out of view on the right. The former priory grounds are now a public park.

DUNSTABLE, *The Town Hall 1897* 39738

A town hall was built in 1805 north of the crossroads; it was replaced by this rather heavy-handed Victorian one in 1879. Demolished in 1966, it has been replaced by offices, while the early 19th-century Crown Inn on the left was replaced by a neo-Georgian one in the 1930s. To the right is a 17th-century archway that once led into the White Horse Inn's coaching yard. Henry VIII once stayed at this inn.

21

▶ **DUNSTABLE**
High Street 1897
39736

Since 1897 there has been much rebuilding on High Street North, particularly on the right-hand side. The grand mid 19th-century rendered post office building (right) went in the 1960s for the uninspiring Quadrant Shopping Centre. The horse drawn bus is passing the Old Sugar Loaf Hotel on the right, a coaching inn with rainwater heads dated 1717 and 1719.

◀ **DUNSTABLE**
Nicholas Way c1965
D69059

The Nicholas Way shopping centre, built in the mid 1960s as part of Dunstable's 'brave new world', was recently refurbished and renamed the Quadrant Shopping Centre. It is sad that the rather impressive clock sculpture has gone, as have the benches and planters. This shows the views into the pedestrian precinct from High Street North towards the north-south parade of shops entered from Church Street.

▲ **DUNSTABLE,** *West Street 1898* 40957

West Street follows the course of the ancient Icknield Way. We are looking past the junction with Victoria Street towards the Watling Street crossroads. The villas on the left have gone; the site is now occupied by 1970s offices, Carlton House. On the right the trees have gone - this is now the entry to St Mary's Gate, a 1960s road with a car park and the 1980s police station on the corner. Much of the building in the distance survives, however, and some of the distant horse chestnuts remain.

◄ **CADDINGTON**
All Saints' Church
c1965 C324015

Caddington, south-east of Dunstable, was sheep country in the Middle Ages, just like Dunstable itself; wool was highly important to the local economy. Some of this wealth was invested in building a fine parish church, whose 15th-century tower has six bells in its belfry. In this view the reset 12th-century Norman south doorway can be seen. The village with its big central green is up on the chalk plateau between the valleys of the Ver and Lea.

LUTON
The Town Hall 1897
39702

Descending into the valley of the Lea, the tour reaches the huge sprawl of Luton, a town which briefly had a castle in the 13th century and grew rapidly in the 19th century, when it was a centre for the straw plaiting and hat industry. This view was taken looking along George Street to the old Town Hall, with Upper George Street to its left and Manchester Street to the right. The early 19th-century Town Hall was replaced by the current one in the 1930s, a grandiose Classical Revival Portland stone building, now offices. The buildings on the right were demolished; the site is now Park Square, with a vast Arndale Centre shopping mall.

LUTON
Vauxhall Motors c1955
L117037

Vauxhall Motors stepped in, moving here from Lambeth in 1905, to replace straw hat making as the major employer in the town. The motor works sprawled east of the town centre with neo-Georgian offices of 1907 (now a business centre) on Kimpton Road behind Frith's photographer. This view shows a service road, with the buildings on the right surviving. Those in the distance have been rebuilt in the 1990s. Vauxhall's activities have now been wound down, and cars are no longer made in Luton. In the distance is the plateau now occupied by Luton Airport.

LUTON, *The Lake, Wardown Park c1960* L117081

Luton's vast suburbs are interspersed with parks, many along the valley of the River Lea; its source is on Leagrave Common, another park, within the town's boundaries. To the north of the town centre the Lea has been dammed to form a lake within the former grounds of Wardown, a mansion of 1875, now Luton Museum and Art Gallery. The park is surrounded by 1930s suburbs, while the lake is now fenced off for a variety of wildfowl. This photograph was taken looking looks towards the delightful iron suspension bridge crossing the lake's waist.

LUTON
Someries Castle 1897
39715

In 1897 the brick-built Someries Castle was tranquil in the middle of open countryside at the head of a dry valley spur from the Lea valley. What remains of Lord Wenlock's 15th-century house is the gatehouse range, seen here from the inner side. There are earthworks and a substantial moat in the fields to the left. Someries seems to be the earliest brick building in Bedfordshire. Its rural idyll is now destroyed by Luton Airport immediately to the north: indeed, the castle is a mere hundred metres from its perimeter fence.

LUTON, *Luton Hoo c1955* L117050

We are a world away from Luton in feel, and yet only just south of the A505 outer ring road. Here on the west side of the Lea valley is the splendid 1760s Capability Brown landscaped park of Luton Hoo, its long lake formed by damming the Lea. Set at the heart of its 1,500 acres is the mansion. Adam worked here (the columned central bow is his), but much was damaged by fire in 1843. The gold and diamond baron, Sir Julius Werner, had it remodelled and transformed by Mewes and Davis around 1903. Open to the public, Luton Hoo is famed for its Russian and European art collection, including much by Fabergé.

▶ **HARPENDEN**
*The Parish Church
c1955*   H25001

The town grew up in the Middle Ages out of Westminster Abbey's gradual clearance of its wooded estates within the manor of Wheathampstead for farming and settlement. The first reference to the parish church was in 1221. Despite appearances, the only medieval part of the church is the west tower of about 1470. The rest was rebuilt in 1862, the arches in alternating white and red stone, a form of polychromy popular in the mid-Victorian period.

◀ **HARPENDEN**
High Street c1960 H25032

The town grew up south of the church. It has a strikingly unusual plan, standing at the north tip of a vast triangular common more than a mile long, now given more definition by 20th-century development along both edges. There are some fine Georgian houses beside the northern part of the common, which narrows down to a tree-lined grassy bank south of the church. This view, though, captures something of the present suburban character of Harpenden, which expanded and became a commuter town after the railway arrived in the later 19th century.

▲ **HARPENDEN,** *The Old Cock Inn c1965* H25066

The road from Luton to St Albans through Harpenden, now the A1081, was turnpiked in 1727; several of the inns prospered from these improvements, including the Old Cock Inn, whose painted brick front of circa 1800 conceals an earlier building. Further south along the High Street, the George has been on the site since at least 1507.

◀ **HARPENDEN**
Rothamsted Research Station c1965 H25067

Further south, this neo-Georgian building looks over the point where the common widens out. The Rothamsted Trust was founded in 1889 by John Bennet Lawes, who had inherited the Rothamsted estate on the outskirts of the town in 1834. Lawes made a fortune in phosphate fertiliser, and set up an experimental station and laboratories in the 1850s. These buildings date from the First World War, and are no longer creeper-clad. The buildings to the right are dated 1923. The stone memorial, erected in 1893, commemorates fifty years of continuous experiments.

HARPENDEN
Rothamsted Park c1955
H25013

Rothamsted Park, hundreds of acres west of the town and much of it walked by the public, is part of the research station, now named the Institute of Arable Crops Research. This view was taken looking along the eastern one of the lime avenues that lead to the mansion from the Hatching Green entrance. The brick house itself has a medieval core, but owes its present appearance to Sir John Wittewronge (his family was originally from Flanders), who between 1638 and 1659 extended, altered and transformed it, even giving it Dutch gables.

REDBOURN, *The Church c1955* R87008

Three miles west of Harpenden is Redbourn, a small town or large village, with its High Street along Watling Street and its church a mile away at the west end of a large triangular green or common. A lime avenue leads through the churchyard to the church, whose west tower is crowned by a spirelet of the 'Hertfordshire spike' type. The nave and tower are Norman, and were consecrated between 1094 and 1119. A Garden of Rest was created in 1956 between the chancel and the north aisle for the interment of cremated ashes – it was enlarged in 1979.

WHIPSNADE, *The Zoo, Bactrian Camels c1960* W299004

The world famous Whipsnade Zoo was the very first open or free-range zoo in Europe at a time when cages were the norm. It was established by the Zoological Society of London, whose London Zoo in Regents Park opened in 1828. A conservation centre from the start, with large animals in relatively natural surroundings, the first animals (pheasants and jungle fowl) arrived in 1928. From this small start the collection grew rapidly, and was opened to the public in 1931. The camels, still popular, are looking content.

▼ **WHIPSNADE,** *The Zoo, Flamingo Island c1960* W299014

A giant chalk-cut lion on the western chalk escarpment is the logo of Whipsnade, which is set in over 600 acres on the Chilterns. The zoo site was previously a derelict farm, Hall Farm, and was bought in 1926 for nearly £13,500, roughly £22.50 per acre: a bargain that has given pleasure to millions over the succeeding years. Its collection now includes over 2,500 animals, ranging from these flamingos to rhinos, tigers and giraffes.

▶ **WHIPSNADE**
The Gap c1960
W299033

This view was taken looking westwards from the western edge of the zoo towards the Ivinghoe Hills in the distance. The row of trees in the middle distance mark the Hemel Hempstead to Leighton Buzzard road, the A4146. This gives a good idea of the steep drop of about 200 feet from the zoo on the plateau into the valley below.

◄ WHIPSNADE
The Parish Church c1960 W299056

The village is located to the east of the zoo; it is a scattered one, with houses and cottages spread along the edges of a very large green. St Mary Magdalene's Parish Church stands on the south side of the green; to the right, westwards, are Church Farm's barns, which have now been converted into dwellings. The church is unusual in that it is all brick. The tower is 16th-century, the nave with its striking arched windows and rusticated doorway is Georgian, while the apse and chancel (left) were rebuilt in 1866.

► EATON BRAY
High Street c1955 E104007

Also in Bedfordshire, Eaton Bray merges with Edlesborough across the Buckinghamshire county boundary. This view was taken looking north-west along the High Street towards the well treed churchyard with its obelisk war memorial. The Victorian terraces on the left survive, but the old vicarage (its grounds are on the right) was rebuilt in the 1960s. Bray was added to the village name after Reginald de Bray was granted the manor in 1490 by Henry VII, upon whose head Reginald had placed Richard III's crown after the Battle of Bosworth.

BERKHAMSTED AND THE HERTFORDSHIRE CHILTERNS

BERKHAMSTED, *High Street c1965* B407115x

The second chapter moves westward into Hertfordshire, where the Roman road known as Akeman Street cut through a gap in the Chilterns; it was followed centuries later by the Grand Junction Canal in the 1790s and the railway in the 1830s. Medieval Berkhamsted grew up along the Roman road, with its Norman castle (the impressive remains stand on the north side of the river Bulbourne) guarding this strategic gap. This view in the High Street along the market place. The buildings on the right are undistinguished; since this view was taken the Waitrose building (left) has been replaced, sad to say.

BERKHAMSTED
The Parish Church c1960
B407044

We are now beyond view B407115x (page 34). Past some market place infill buildings just out of shot to the left, known delightfully as Grab All Row, lies the large and heavily restored parish church of St Peter, its long south front alongside the High Street. The large central tower is of about 1200; the belfry was added in 1335 - the work was paid for by John and Alyce Phylypp, according to a now illegible inscription stone. Of the cars seen here, only the Morris Minor on the right is still much seen nowadays.

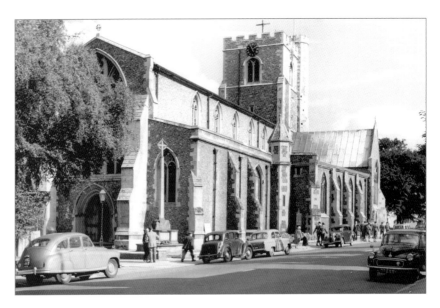

BERKHAMSTED, *School House c1960* B407047

Apart from traffic jams on the A41 (until the dual carriageway by-pass was built in the 1990s), the town was best known for its public school. It started life in Tudor times as a grammar school for local boys, and over time became less and less 'public'. It was founded by a local boy made good, John Incent, Dean of St Paul's, in about 1541, and what is now School House was built in about 1544. The great hall windows can be seen beyond the war memorial in this view, which looks north down Castle Street from beside the church.

36

BERKHAMSTED, *Ashridge College c1965* B407095

Up on the chalk ridge beyond the wooded Berkhamsted Common
and about three miles from the town lies Ashridge, a chalk stone
mansion in medieval style encrusted with battlements. Designed
for the Duke of Bridgewater by James Wyatt in 1808, with additions
up to 1820 by his son Jeffrey (who Frenchified his name to
Wyatville), it is now a college, and looks north-west towards a golf
course. Much of the Ashridge estate, some 4,000 acres, has been
given to the National Trust; these former commons are heavily
wooded, and interlaced by attractive well-walked paths and rides.

TRING, *The Parish Church c1960* T81033

Tring, at the Chiltern end of a salient of Hertfordshire that projects into Buckinghamshire, lies on Akeman Street, the former Roman road through the Chilterns. Long ago the road was diverted north through the High Street around the area where Tring Park grew up. The town was granted a market charter in 1315. The parish church of St Peter and St Paul can be viewed from the High Street across a square; since 1992 there has been a maze here featuring a zebra's head, a reference to the town's Zoological Museum. The church is notable for the extraordinarily grandiose 1707 monument inside to Sir William Gore of Tring Park, once Lord Mayor of London.

TRING
The Rose and Crown Hotel c1955
T81301

Members of the Rothschild banking family bought themselves country houses in Buckinghamshire (Waddesdon and Mentmore, for instance), and in Hertfordshire Nathan Meyer, later Lord Rothschild, acquired Tring Park. He also set about improving the town itself, and rebuilt and added many buildings in Tudor 'Old English' style. The Georgian Rose and Crown in the High Street was demolished and replaced by this grandiose Rothschildean image of a coaching inn in 1905. Since this view was taken, the carriageway has been built in to form an entrance lobby, but otherwise the building is virtually unchanged.

TRING, *Tring Park 1897* 39649

Tring Park and its estate was bought by Lionel Rothschild in 1872 and passed to his son Nathan Meyer on his death in 1879. Although the mansion looks 19th-century French, the Rothschild pavilion roof and other embellishments conceal a house designed by Sir Christopher Wren in the late 1670s. Indeed, the house is set in superb 18th century parkland, somewhat spoilt by the A41 Tring by-pass that cuts it in two unequal sections - the house stands in the smaller northern part. The mansion is now the Arts Educational School, which focuses on education of children in the performing arts.

TRING, *The Museum, Ground Floor c1955* T81029

The Walter Rothschild Zoological Museum to the west of the mansion is entered from Akeman Street, and contains a remarkable collection of stuffed animals set out in their Victorian glass display cases. Admission is free, and the collection is housed in buildings erected by the Rothschilds in 1889 and later. This photograph was taken in the ground floor Gallery 1: a friendly looking polar bear greets the visitor.

TRING
The Museum, Top Floor
c1955 T81028

The basis of the museum was a remarkable 21st birthday present from Baron Meyer to his son Walter in 1889. Already an avid collector of specimens, Walter added greatly to the collection. In the 1930s Walter (by then the second Baron Rothschild) gave it to the British Museum before his death; it is now a branch of the Natural History Museum, itself a branch of the British Museum. This view is in Gallery 5 on the upper floor, with marine mammals on the right; a giant Elephant Seal is perched atop the display case.

BOVINGDON, *High Street and the Ryder Memorial c1965* B409012

Heading for Hemel Hempstead, this short tour passes through Bovingdon south-west of the town on the Chesham Road (the B4505). It is a much-expanded village with occasional pockets of character. This view was taken looking north-west past the pond and the junction with Green Lane on the left. The well-house with its pyramidal roof was built in 1881 in memory of the then lord of the manor, Granville Dudley Ryder. In the 19th century, the well was where Luton straw was brought for the home workers to collect and plait. It was then collected and used in the Luton straw hat industry.

▶ **HEMEL HEMPSTEAD**
St Mary's Church c1955 H255008

The old town grew up along the east side of the Gade valley. The High Street undulates along the slopes, with the church lower down and west of the High Street. The town retains many good buildings and houses, but the parish church is quite outstanding. It is almost entirely Norman of the 12th century, with aisles, transepts and a fine central tower. Only the porches and vestries are later, as well as most of the windows, and of course the tall, elegant lead-clad spire which soars over 200 feet.

▼ **HEMEL HEMPSTEAD**
View from Adeyfield Road c1955 H255017

Hemel Hempstead was to change irrevocably in the 1950s: it was designated a 'New Town' in 1947 under the New Town Act 1946. To the left of this view the new town was already growing rapidly, and it would shortly occupy the hills on the far side of the Gade valley beyond the church. Here Frith's photographer looks north-west across 1950s and earlier housing towards the old town with its church and spire; he was standing in Adeyfield Road, whose semis continue downhill on the left to meet St Paul's Road.

HEMEL HEMPSTEAD, *Chaulden, The Shopping Centre c1965* H255090

To most people, however, Hemel Hempstead is a vast modern town with one of the most complicated roundabouts in England, and infilling the space between the M1 and the A41 with seas of housing estates. This is unfair, for the New Town Act towns were carefully planned. Hemel works well with the hilly topography, allowing the concept of local centres with their own churches, schools, pubs and shops to give a sense of local identity. This view shows the shopping crescent in Chaulden from the roof of the pub, the Tudor Rose. Chaulden is a 'neighbourhood community' on the west of the River Gade.

HEMEL HEMPSTEAD
The Town Centre c1960
H255027

The centre of the new town took its cue from the old town and its relationship to the River Gade valley. Laid out to its south by Geoffrey Jellicoe, the planning consultant, it used the river similarly as its western boundary. This view was taken looking from the riverside road, Waterhouse Street, into Bank Place and towards the main street, which is now pedestrianised. The fountain has gone, but the banks remain. The offices topped by a clock-tower have been replaced by the Mayflower Shopping Centre. This view gives a good idea of the quality of late 1950s architecture.

► **HEMEL HEMPSTEAD**
The Rock and Roll Statue and the Water Garden c1963 H255041

The Gade was carefully landscaped along Waterhouse Street, and a park was created on the west bank. This view shows the wires beyond the bridge used for espaliering lime trees; these are now mature, of course, and a delightful feature in the townscape. The new hedge beyond the bench (left) has also matured to conceal the car park. To the right are the buildings of the town centre (view H255027, page 43). The rock and roll statue set in the river struck a contemporary note when it was installed in 1962.

◄ **HEMEL HEMPSTEAD**
The Pavilion c1965
H255150

This view in Marlowes, the continuation of the main shopping street of the new town, was taken looking northwards past the junction with Combe Street, with one of the older buildings in the distance, the Marlowes Methodist Church (right). The cinema with its Presto café survives, but it is now a pub, the Full House, a punning reference to the old Odeon. The Pavilion beyond was demolished in 2003, and beyond it are the council offices, here concealed. The 1960s building beyond the bus (right) is now West Herts College's Dacorum Campus.

AMERSHAM AND THE SOUTHERN BUCKINGHAMSHIRE CHILTERNS

AMERSHAM, *The View from Rectory Woods c1955* A148171

Our tour moves westwards into the Buckinghamshire Chilterns, and starts in Amersham, one of the most attractive and historic market towns in the Chilterns. It grew up in the River Misbourne valley. Here Frith's photographer looks south downhill from the edge of Rectory Woods to an almost unchanged view, with the parish church in the centre. The incongruous tower block to its right was built as a nurses' home for Amersham Hospital in the mid 1960s; we may be thankful that it has recently been demolished.

AMERSHAM
The Parish Church
c1955   A148047

This view of the large, heavily restored parish church was taken from the Memorial Gardens. The 15th-century west tower to this prosperous town church had the picturesque octagonal spired stair turret top added in 1888. Inside the church are many fine monuments, many of them to the Drake family of Shardeloes, the lords of the manor, and in the 19th century the preservers of the town's historic core (see view A148020, page 49).

AMERSHAM, *The Garden of Remembrance c1955*   A148048

The Memorial Gardens were created in 1949 to commemorate the dead of Amersham in two World Wars; the 1921 First World War memorial cross was relocated here from the churchyard. A row of cottages had been demolished in 1939 (Church Row, fronting the Broadway, 17th- and 18th-century infill of part of the old market place), and this allowed the garden to run north from the Broadway and to be seen from there. The fountain has since been replaced by a smaller stone one.

▶ **AMERSHAM**
General View c1960
A148070

This photograph across the roof tops shows the view along Broadway across the Memorial Gardens towards the High Street, past the Market Hall with its white-painted clock-tower cupola (centre). This dates from 1682, and was built by Sir William Drake of Shardeloes for the town. The building on the left with a lantern to its slate roof is the Lower Baptist Meeting House of 1783, a counterpoint to the much older parish church. In the distance (right) in this virtually unchanged view is Shardeloes (view A148020, page 49), lying in the lee of the far ridge.

◀ **AMERSHAM**
The River Misbourne c1960
A148124

The River Misbourne runs along the north side of the town and passes under Church Street. This apparently rural view was taken looking west from beside the Victorian expansion of St Mary's churchyard, just out of view to the right. Glimpsed through the trees are the buildings of the old Weller's brewery, later the Goya perfume factory, and since 1988 converted to flats. To the left is now the garden of the new rectory, a distinctive pyramidal-roofed house of 1985 designed by Sir Basil Spence, who is more famous for designing Coventry Cathedral.

▲ **AMERSHAM,** *Shardeloes c1950* A148020

To the west of the town lies Shardeloes (left of photograph), the home of the Drake family, later the Tyrwhitt-Drakes, who as lords of the manor and principal landowners kept the Victorian railway boom at bay and thus preserved the town and its setting amid the Chiltern hills. The 17th-century house was rebuilt by Stiff Leadbetter and Robert Adam in the 1750s and 1760s. The stable block to the right of the house dates from the 1720s. This view was taken from the dual carriageway on the A413, the successor to the old road; this had been shifted north so that Drake could form an ornamental lake in the Misbourne valley.

◀ **AMERSHAM ON THE HILL**
Station Road c1960
A373093

When the railway was finally allowed to come, it ran well north of the old town on the ridge of the hills and out of sight of Shardeloes. The Metropolitan railway station opened in 1892, and Amersham on the Hill grew up, in effect a new town, separated from the old town by woods and fields on the valley sides. This view shows Station Road, a mere cart track before 1892; the road descends towards the Misbourne valley, with houses set behind trees and leafy hedges.

AMERSHAM ON THE HILL
Chesham Road c1955
A373085

Up in Amersham on the Hill, Oakfield Corner, built around 1910, stands at the junction with Chesham Road. To the left is Rectory Hill, until the 1890s the only way up from the old town. The traffic lights have now been replaced by mini-roundabouts, and the site on the left, Oakfield Close, was redeveloped for housing in the 1990s. Oakfield Corner is built in the timber-framed style so popular in suburban shopping centres around 1900; it was later supplanted by sash-windowed neo-Georgian after the First World War.

▶ **AMERSHAM ON THE HILL**
Oakfield Corner
c1960 A373096

This view was taken looking south past Oakfield Corner into Hill Avenue, which leads to the railway station, the raison d'etre for Amersham on the Hill. The station was opened in September 1892, and immediately became a popular commuter station for London workers. Indeed, the Metropolitan Railway was itself a developer, and laid out estates (such as Elm Close) near the station. This view captures well the somewhat amorphous and piecemeal nature of the new town's commercial architecture.

◀ **LITTLE MISSENDEN**
The Manor House c1955
L350010

West of Amersham, also in the Misbourne valley, Little Missenden is a compact and very pretty village grouped around a crossroads. Its centrepiece is the Manor House. It stands to the east of the very fine and unspoilt parish church of St John the Baptist, which is noted for its medieval wall paintings. The yews of the churchyard can be seen to the left in this view. The Manor House's oldest part is the 16th-century timber-framed wing at the right, while the larger brick part is mostly late 17th-century. Note the many and varied chimneys.

▲ **LITTLE MISSENDEN,** *The White Cottage c1955* L350015

Turning his back on the Manor House, Frith's photographer now looked down the lane which leads to Holmer Green. The White Cottage (left) is a 17th-century timber-framed house which has been refronted with fake framing added. Since this view it has been extended by a further gabled bay, replacing the lean-to. Town Farm Cottage beyond also has fake timber-framed bays - the two farthest ones are modern additions. In the distance is Breaches Wood, a typical Chiltern beechwood 'hanger'.

◀ **LITTLE MISSENDEN**
*The River Misbourne
c1955* L350008

Now north of the crossroads, the photographer looked east from the bridge over the Misbourne along the rear of Manor Farm towards the Red Lion pub (the tall hipped roof, centre right) and the cottages beyond. This view is much changed following the conversion of the barns to houses in the 1980s. The cattle-grazed field is now a trans-riverine garden to a converted barn, and the pub has been smartened up, and includes a riverside terrace.

◀ **GREAT MISSENDEN**
The Parish Church c1955
G241043

Moving westward along the valley with its sparkling clear stream, the tour reaches Great Missenden. This small town grew up at the gates of Missenden Abbey, which had been founded in about 1133. The town lies west of the Misbourne, with its High Street on the old Aylesbury road. The abbey occupies the valley floor, with the church above on the eastern slopes well away from the town; the building is mostly 14th- and 15th-century. Today, there is a burial ground extension in the left foreground and a car park to the right.

◄ LITTLE MISSENDEN
Missenden House c1955
L350005

East of the village crossroads and beyond the pub, Missenden House is the other architecturally 'polite' house in the village. Set in its own grounds behind ball-finialled gate piers and walls, it is dated 1729 on a rainwater head. With full-height bay windows flanking the central doorway, it is a fine early Georgian composition, with box sash windows and a moulded brick cornice below its parapet.

▲ **GREAT MISSENDEN,** *From the Church Tower c1955* G241036

The isolation of the church east of the town is now even more emphasised by the A413 by-pass, which runs between the church and the town on the slopes of the east bank of the Misbourne. Made in the late 1950s, the by-pass cuts across the trees and the field in the foreground; access to the church is over a bridge. Church Lane leads to a green with the 1870s school (right). The High Street is beyond, with suburban housing climbing the well-treed hill to the left - the railway's arrival in 1892 spawned this growth. The big trees to the left foreground mark the boundary of Missenden Abbey's grounds.

◄ GREAT MISSENDEN
Missenden Abbey c1955 G241045

The medieval abbey was founded in 1133 by William de Missenden. After its dissolution under Henry VIII in 1538, some of its buildings survived to become a mansion; this incorporated some of the monastic buildings around the cloister, although the abbey church was totally demolished. The grounds were landscaped in the 1770s, including the fine lake, and the late Georgian house was medievalised after 1815. There was a superb 15th-century roof to the dorter, but all this was destroyed by fire in 1985. Now a college and conference centre, the building was carefully restored; this view is little changed.

▼ **CHESHAM,** *The Parish Church 1897* 40540

The route now climbs out of the Misbourne valley and then descends into the Chess Valley. Like the Misbourne, the Chess, another pretty Chiltern stream, flows south-east to join the River Colne. This late Victorian view was taken looking across the Chess from Germain Street and the water meadow towards the backs of Church Street houses, with the crossing tower and spirelet of St Mary's Parish Church beyond. This view is now obscured by a laurel hedge that screens the 1980s Water Meadow Car Park, although one of the horse chestnut trees on the left survives.

► **CHESHAM**
Market Square c1970 C81088

Chesham grew up in the narrow valley cut between the chalk ridges. The immediate hills on either side remain undeveloped, and the town fans out to the north; this expansion occurred mainly after the Metropolitan Railway branch line to Chesham opened in 1889. This view was taken looking north along the Market Square towards the High Street, and shows a road 'improvement', for the old town hall was until 1968 to the left of the traffic island. Rebuilt in 1856, it was unnecessarily demolished; but as a sop a clock tower was reinstated on its site in 1992, utilising the original clock.

◄ **CHESHAM**
High Street c1955
C81004

Moving north, the photographer looked south from The Broadway into the High Street. At the left, by the 1898 bank (which is now a pub), is Station Road; this was laid out around 1889, when the railway arrived up the valley. The low buildings beyond Boots (centre) have been rebuilt, as have most of those on the right, including the Lamb pub, which went in 1974. Their replacements in some cases are utterly awful examples of 1960s brutalism and disregard for their surroundings.

► **CHESHAM**
The Broadway 1921 70540

This photograph was taken just before the war memorial, with its figure of a soldier leaning on his rifle, replaced the horse trough and ornate gas lamp later that same year. On the left Weatherill's is still a chemist, albeit with a modern shopfront, but the Chesham Palace cinema next door, later the Astoria, went in the 1970s. The high building at the corner of Station Road beyond the signpost was an International Stores and Club and Literary Institute. It was built as a temperance hotel in the 1890s to serve commercial travellers using the railway, and is now a night club.

► **CHESHAM**
Missenden Road
1921 70550

Leaving Chesham along Church Street, a street with the town's best cottages fronting its winding course, we cross the young River Chess, which passes under the road and is railed off to the right. Much is changed in this view. The timber-framed cottages have been cleared for road improvement, and in the distance (centre) is now the entrance to Dawes Close, old people's bungalows built in 1959 under a trust created by Mary Gertrude Dawes. The houses and cottages on the right survive.

◄ **CHESHAM**
Stanley Avenue 1906 53652

When the railway arrived in 1889 the expansion of the town got under way, although there had been much 19th-century building along Broad Street in the valley north of the old town centre. Much of this was terraced artisan dwellings for industrial workers, but after 1889 the northern suburbs expanded to north-east and north-west. This view shows one of these commuter and middle-class roads. Stanley Avenue was laid out in the 1890s and is remarkably little changed today, apart from the loss of most of the iron railings. Most of the trees survive.

▲ **CHESHAM,** *Waterside 1897* 40546

By the time the Chess leaves Chesham, it is quite broad and running in a flat-bottomed valley. Waterside follows the north bank of the river; it grew in the 19th century, with watermills, workshops, small factories and workers' cottages in considerable numbers. This view was taken looking across towards Christ Church, which was built in the 1860s to serve this community. The tall chimneys of the former vicarage rise on the left skyline, but the old school to the right of the church has now been replaced by housing. The industrial buildings on the left have gone, replaced in the 1960s by three-storey blocks of flats, Riverside Court.

◀ **CHESHAM BOIS**
Bois Lane c1955 C693009

Chesham Bois is situated on the chalk plateau south of Chesham, and now merges with Amersham on the Hill to the immediate south. There is a medieval church half a mile north of the common, but the overwhelming character is of prosperous Metroland houses and villas in big gardens along well-treed roads. This shows the view looking north along Bois Lane from beside South Road, which skirts the south side of the tree-covered common to the left. To the right is Chestnut Lane, and behind the tree (now gone) stands the flint-built Old School House, now extended and a dwelling.

LATIMER
From the South c1960
L504007

Our route descends again into the Chess valley. The river was once noted for its high quality watercress, but now only one commercial cress-bed survives near Chenies. This is the view looking north across the Chess valley from Walk Wood beside Stony Lane into Flaunden Bottom, a scenic dry valley that joins the main valley at Latimer - the edge of the village is in the middle distance. The woods in the foreground have just been replanted in this 1960 view, but are now grown to maturity; there is also more woodland descending the slopes towards the farmstead in the middle distance.

LATIMER, *The Village c1960* L504009

Latimer lies on the north slopes of the Chess valley. There is a small village green at its east end surrounded by 17th-century timber-framed cottages (such as Foliots to the left), 19th-century estate cottages and a school. Latimer House is uphill to the west. The green has a roofed parish pump (right) and an obelisk memorial to the Boer War - the then Lord Chesham of Latimer House was a Brigadier-General in that war. In front a horse, Villebois, is buried; it was wounded in the Boer War and brought back to England by Lord Chesham, dying in 1911.

LATIMER
The River Chess c1960
L504002

The river is noted for its brown trout – there are many in the dammed sections within the landscaped grounds of Latimer House. This is the view looking east from the road bridge on the road into Latimer. Most of the railings on the right have been replaced by ubiquitous post and wire fencing. Beyond the single tree, in the copse to its left in the distance, is the site of Flaunden's parish church, partly still standing in 1910 but now virtually vanished. The church was built in about 1230, and the village was moved uphill by Lord Latimer in the late 18th century.

CHENIES, *The Manor House c1955* C609036

Chenies, a mile further downstream along the Chess, takes its name from the Cheyne family. They held the manor from the 13th century until the 16th, when it passed through marriage to the Russells, later Earls and Dukes of Bedford. The older part of its superb brick-built manor house, concealed by the lime tree's bright spring foliage, is 15th-century, while the left-hand range with the crow-step gable was added by 1530 for Sir John Russell, later Earl of Bedford, as a lodgings range for distinguished guests - these included Queen Elizabeth I.

CHENIES
The Parish Church 1897
39681

The medieval church alongside the manor house drive remains the Russell family mausoleum. They added a private chapel in 1556 north of the chancel, much rebuilt and enlarged since, in which repose a quite splendid collection of their effigies and monuments from the 16th century to the present day. This is a heavily restored church; some of the work of the 1887 restoration is evident in this Victorian photograph (the other restoration was in 1861). The bleakness is relieved by a number of trees nowadays, mainly limes, that flank the drive to the manor house.

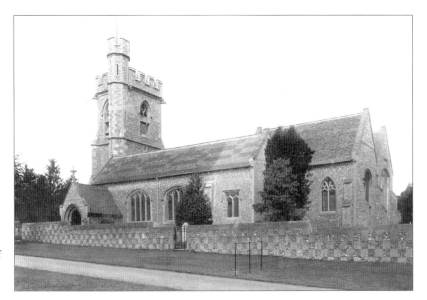

CHENIES, *The Village c1955* C609013

Although there are a few older cottages, Chenies village is basically the creation of the Dukes of Bedford, with the majority of cottages dating from the 1820s, 1840s and 1850s in their estate style: brick, simplified Tudor detail and lattice leaded windows. This view is of the east part of the village, looking along the lane back towards the village green, which is at the manor house end. Here we see 18th- and 19th-century cottages, with 1840s Bedford estate cottages beyond the bus stop. The left-hand trees went to make a wider verge some years later.

CHENIES
The Red Lion Hotel c1955
C609014

Here Frith's photographer looked in the opposite direction to view C609013 (page 62) past the Red Lion, an early 19th-century pub with its attractive bay windows, towards the Baptist chapel with its round-arched windows. The chapel was built in the 1770s and enlarged in 1799; its frontage railings date from 1840. It is a delightful brick building, its hipped roof covered with slate; inside there are galleries on three sides, lit by upper windows. The trees and hedges on the right in this view went to create a wider grass verge.

CHALFONT ST GILES, *The Village c1965* C498042

Our tour crosses the chalk hills south-west of Chenies to rejoin the Misbourne valley south of Amersham at Chalfont St Giles. This village is on the west side of the river, with the main Amersham road, the A413, running along the east side of the valley. It has certainly fared much better in keeping its old buildings and character than its neighbour Chalfont St Peter. It has a charming pond, then a small village green with the parish church tower behind (left); the High Street is lined with good buildings, many of them 17th-century and timber-framed, and the scale is near perfect.

▶ **CHALFONT ST GILES**
The Parish Church and the War Memorial c1955
C498012

St Giles's Church sits in a delightful churchyard with the backs of the old High Street and The Green houses along its west side; to the east the River Misbourne runs in its valley. Heavily restored and refaced outside, the church retains much more character inside. There are important 14th-century wall paintings, and the monuments are good, particularly the one to Sir George Fleetwood, who died in 1620, and his wife. The war memorial looks pristine here – it had recently been cleaned when the Second World War names were added.

◀ **CHALFONT ST GILES**
High Street c1955 C498014

Frith's photographer was now beside the junction with Bowstridge Lane, looking east down the High Street towards the green in the middle distance. On the left are the heavily buttressed walls to the grounds of the old rectory; on the right the bakery (advertising Daren Bread, Lyons Cakes and Hovis) is still a bakery, and the butcher's beyond, A Warner, is still a butcher's. The 19th-century facade of Church Farm Stores with its three gables (right) conceals a timber-framed building, in which remains of late16th-century wall paintings were found during 1980s repairs.

▲ **COLESHILL,** *The Pond c1965* C496010

The last village we visit on our way back to Amersham is situated on the chalk plateau about a mile and a half south of the town and west of the Beaconsfield road, the A355. Coleshill is particularly interesting historically, as it was an enclave of Hertfordshire surrounded by Buckinghamshire. Coleshill was incorporated into Buckinghamshire only in 1844; until then it had been part of Hertfordshire's Dacorum Hundred and attached to Tring, over ten miles away. This is even more curious, as it seems likely that it was upland pasture for Tring's flocks and herds.

◀ **COLESHILL**
The Village c1965 C496004

This second view in Coleshill was taken looking past the shops (visible in view C496010 across the pond) northwards towards the parish church - one shop is now a house, helpfully renamed The Old Stores. An old chapel of ease was demolished around 1800, and the parish had to wait until 1860 for G E Street to design the rather ordinary small Victorian Chiltern church (centre left). As an enclave outside Buckinghamshire, Coleshill had long been popular for gatherings of Dissenters, so the new church was an attempt to bring the village back into the Anglican fold.

COLESHILL, *The Common c1960* C496001

The village pond lies at the tip of the triangular common, which runs south from it with a lane on all three sides. This view looks south-west from beside Windmill Hill. The common is by no means flat, and drops by about 60 feet from north to south. In the distance is the wooded ridge that skirts north of Beaconsfield and Penn. The area in the foreground is nowadays more scrubby and gorse-covered, but the pasture beyond is still grazed.

COLESHILL, *The Windmill c1965* C496012

Windmill Hill is so named because on its east side stands Grove Mill. It looks pretty sorry for itself in this 1960s view, but it has since been restored, and is now complete with its sails, cap and fantail. This tower mill was built in 1856; the foreground is now occupied by a substantial extension. Windmills were once numerous, but few survive in the Chilterns. Survivors include Cobstone, Above Turville, Cholesbury, Lacey Green and Pitstone. All have been brought back from the brink of collapse, Lacey Green's appropriately enough by the Chiltern Society.

HIGH WYCOMBE AND THE WESTERN BUCKINGHAMSHIRE CHILTERNS

HIGH WYCOMBE, *From the South 1921* 70599

This fourth tour starts in what is now the largest town in the Buckinghamshire Chilterns. Its origins were as a corn market centre, but it changed in the 19th century into a major furniture making centre, using the Chiltern beech woods for its raw materials. In this view we can see the chimneys of furniture factories and workshops. The view was taken from Tom Burt's Hill, looking past Loakes House (now converted to flats), probably built as a dower house to Wycombe Abbey. Beyond is a school of 1914. The hills beyond are more built up today, and the parish church (centre) is a little obscured by the six-storey 1950s Buckinghamshire Chilterns University College.

69

► **HIGH WYCOMBE**
The Rye c1955
H84015

Frith's photographer looked, across The Rye, now a park, but formerly pasture for the town's cattle. The water in the foreground is The Dyke, a long lake which was formed by damming the River Wye upstream. It was within the grounds of Wycombe Abbey until it was given to the town in 1923 by Lord Carrington as a memorial to his son, Viscount Wendover, killed in France during the First World War. The villas front London Road; behind is artisan housing and furniture workshops and factories. By the 1950s, housing had spread over the northern hills.

◄ **HIGH WYCOMBE**
All Saints' Parish Church c1955
H84038

Wycombers will tell you that All Saints' is the largest parish church in Buckinghamshire; it is the centrepiece of the town. Originally the church had a central tower, but this was taken down and the church altered in 1509-1510. Between 1521 and 1535 the west tower was built - it is similar to the contemporary one at St Mary's in Henley (view H73007, page 105). The cornice and parapets were added in 1755 by Henry Keene. He also designed the nearby Guildhall for the Earl of Shelburne, who lived at Loakes Manor (later renamed Wycombe Abbey – see H84028, page 71).

▲ **HIGH WYCOMBE,** *Wycombe Abbey School c1955* H84028

Wycombe Abbey lies immediately south of the town, and is set in grounds landscaped in consultation with the great Capability Brown in the 1760s. At that time it was owned by the Earl of Shelburne (who had been Prime Minister for a year) and was called Loakes Manor. Henry Keene added a block to the 17th-century brick house. Then in 1798 the banker Robert Smith (later ennobled as Lord Carrington) bought the estate, and employed James Wyatt to transform it into a Gothic mansion, at the same time renaming it the far more romantic Wycombe Abbey. His successors sold the house, and it became a pioneering girls' school in 1896.

◄ **HIGH WYCOMBE**
Wycombe Abbey School Grounds c1965 H84122

The school also bought many acres of the grounds. Lord Carrington moved uphill to Daws Hill House, the home farm, which he transformed into a stylish residence (now also owned by the school). The school commissioned a leading architect of the day, W D Caroe, to design school buildings. These included a fine chapel in 1926 and these boarding houses which back onto Marlow Hill, built between 1898 and 1902. The school is now one of the country's leading girls' public schools.

HIGH WYCOMBE
Langley Vale and the Abbey Grounds c1960 H84075

The school grounds are an invaluable green lung to the town, which occupies the valley of the River Wye - the other surrounding hills have been built over almost completely. This view was taken looking down Langley Vale (which is rented out for cattle grazing) towards the school, whose main building can be seen in the centre distance. The railway can be seen beyond, with the Victorian and Edwardian villas climbing Amersham Hill on either side of the straight road (centre); the far hills are now covered in housing.

WEST WYCOMBE, *High Street c1955* W340002

About three miles west of High Wycombe, also on the London to Oxford road (the A40), is a complete contrast: the village of West Wycombe. Its High Street is one of the finest and least altered in the Chilterns, a state that will continue, for the Dashwoods of West Wycombe sold the village to the Royal Society of Arts in 1929. They in turn sold it to the National Trust in 1934, thus ensuring its future. This view was taken looking east along the High Street. The finest timber-framed building is Church Loft with its clock (right), which was built in the late 15th century as four lock-up shops with an open hall above.

WEST WYCOMBE
Church Lane c1960 W340019

Church Lane leads uphill from the High Street - it is the only side street in the old village. Here the photographer looked downhill towards the High Street, with the back of the 15th-century Church Loft extending over the lane. To its right is the flint and brick former Wesleyan Methodist chapel with an inscribed tile 'I Bigg, Mason 1815'. It is now a Christadelphian Ecclesia. Mellow brick 18th- and 19th-century cottages climb the hill; the further one with the dormer is dated 1722. On the left are the grounds of the old vicarage, a mid 16th-century timber-framed house.

WEST WYCOMBE, *The George and Dragon c1955* W340008

Back in the High Street, the 18th-century George and Dragon is West Wycombe's only coaching inn still a pub. Its curiously slab-like tall frontage dominates the street. Next door but one, beyond the white-fronted building, was the Black Boy Inn, but it is now an architect's office and a cane and rush furniture restoration workshop. Further on is the Swan, one of two other surviving pubs in the village. To the right is The Manor House with its elegant lamp bracket.

► **WEST WYCOMBE**
High Street c1955
W340007

We are now further west, with views of the open countryside beyond the village. The Swan is on the left, and one of the few modern buildings is on the right: the former Methodist church of 1894, now offices. Beyond is Aston House, now also offices, including that of the Child Bereavement Trust. To the right of the former church is The Apple Orchard, a 17th-century timber-framed building with a jettied upper floor. An antique shop in the 1950s, it now sells fine furniture and 'unusual gifts'.

◄ **WEST WYCOMBE**
The View from Church Hill c1960
W340010

To the north of the village is a ridge with the earthworks of an Iron Age hill-fort. A more interesting monument is the parish church of St Lawrence, which was largely rebuilt by Francis Dashwood in Georgian style in the 1750s and 1760s. To its east is the great Mausoleum by John Bastard built in the 1760s, an unroofed six-sided structure with columns and entablature, also commissioned by Francis Dashwood – he was the founder of the notorious Hell-Fire Club, and the owner of West Wycombe Park. Here we look towards High Wycombe from beside the Mausoleum along the road Dashwood had made to by-pass his park in the 1750s.

▲ **RADNAGE,** *The Church and Bledlow Ridge c1955* R415007

Moving west into the remoter Chiltern hills, the tour reaches Radnage, a parish of scattered hamlets or 'ends' and farmsteads set in winding narrow lanes. Its parish church sits in isolation on the edge of one of the valleys, with only the 18th-century former rectory for company (left). This view was taken across the valley from Sprigs Holly Lane. St Mary's Church, which serves this scattered community, was built around 1200; it remains aisleless and austere, although the nave was lengthened in the 15th century. Behind are the wooded slopes of Bledlow Ridge.

◄ **HUGHENDEN**
Hughenden Manor c1955 H471001

This chapter's tour now circles north of High Wycombe, crossing the chalk ridges to Hughenden, another parish with no village centre. High on the ridge to the west of the Hughenden valley, the manor and its park effectively stems the tide of housing spreading north from High Wycombe. The largely 18th-century house was bought by Benjamin Disraeli in 1847. His father, Isaac, had rented nearby Bradenham Manor in the 1830s and 1840s, so Benjamin knew the area well; the great British Prime Minister and novelist set about transforming the Georgian house. He used Edward Buckton Lamb, whose quirky work gave it its present character. Here we see the south front.

◄ **HAZLEMERE**
Inkerman Hill c1960
H470003

The next few views are north-east
of High Wycombe, where modern
development merges at Hazlemere,
Tylers Green and Holmer Green.
This view was taken looking south-
west downhill along the Amersham
road, the A404, towards Hazlemere.
Apart from road improvements
and some infill houses in the
distance on Eastern Dene, the view
is unchanged; but the fields on the
left are now part of the Hazlemere
Golf Club, which at least preserves
them as open countryside. The
beech hanger on the distant
ridge survives, and separates two
stretches of modern development.

◄ **HUGHENDEN**
Hughenden Manor,
the Stables c1960
H471004

East of the house is
the stable courtyard;
this side is in plain mid
19th-century style,
although Lamb gave
it a characteristically
odd facade towards
the house. Given to
the National Trust
in 1946, the house is
now partly open to the
public and partly the
Trust's regional offices.
This view was taken
looking through Lamb's
south archway into the
stable courtyard, an
unchanged view, but
no longer stables. The
range on the left is a
shop with the estate
office above, and out
of sight on the right is
the restaurant, restored
after a fire in the late
1990s. Paying visitors
enter though the far
archway.

▲ **HAZLEMERE,** *The Cross Roads c1955* H470010

The main crossroads in Hazlemere has typical piecemeal suburban shopping development,
as well as an older building - the 19th-century Three Horseshoes pub beyond the now
felled conifer (centre left). The building behind the Morris van, Market Parade (centre),
is just finished in this view, while Mannings and Hazlemere post office (right) is still a
newsagent's and post office, part of the Forbuoys chain. Above Stocktons (still a butcher's,
now R S Troutt), is a Greek restaurant, and the chemist at the far right is now a Chinese
takeaway. The busy junctions have been improved by mini-roundabouts.

◄ **HAZLEMERE**
The Crown Hotel c1955
H470005

Nearer High Wycombe on
the Amersham Road, the mid
19th-century Crown is now
flanked by modern housing.
Apart from the eaves, it is
almost entirely built of local
unknapped flint rubble, a
technique popular in the area,
as against the more usual use
of flint for walling and brick
for window and door jambs
and arches. The Crown is
almost unchanged except for
the garage at the right, which
is now converted into a bar
extension. The whole of the
front area is a car park.

▼ **TYLERS GREEN,** *The Horse and Groom c1960* T354011

South-east of Hazlemere the road heads towards Beaconsfield via Tylers Green and Penn, leaving Hazlemere's housing estates behind. This photograph shows the view north along Elm Road at the north end of Tylers Green village; here the common reaches the road at Rays Lane in the dense tree cover to the left. The Horse and Groom closed in 2002, while the Old Bakehouse beyond has been extended. The building on the right is the former coach house to Yonder Lodge, a stuccoed late 18th-century house.

► **TYLERS GREEN**
Elm Road c1955 T354007

As its name suggests, Tylers Green was once a centre for a floor and roof tile industry. Indeed, in the Middle Ages its decorative floor tiles were in great demand, and were used at Windsor Castle in the 14th century. They can still be found on the floors of numerous Chiltern parish churches. Frith's photographer looked north towards the Horse and Groom pub (see view T354011); on the left are the old elms that gave the road its name. Now long killed off by Dutch elm disease, they have been replaced by limes and beech trees.

◀ **TYLERS GREEN**
The Green c1955
T354006

The pretty triangular village green at the School Road and Elm Road junction has a large pond, now more reedy. This view was taken looking westwards, with the 1875 school with its pretty bellcote (now Tylers Green First School) by the High Wycombe architect Arthur Vernon on the left. In the distance is the tower of St Margaret's Parish Church, the tower an addition by Arthur Vernon in 1891 to the 1854 church. In the centre of the view is the former St Margaret's Working Men's Club, built in 1878 and also by Arthur Vernon; it was provided for the village by Sir Philip Rose of nearby Rayners. It is now a private house.

▶ **PENN**
The Parish Church c1955
P283003

From Tylers Green, the main street of Penn village, Church Road, runs eastward along a ridge to the parish church of Holy Trinity. In such a wealthy village it is a surprise to find a church so unspoilt by restoration. Since this view was taken the last areas of render have been removed to expose the flint rubble walls, and the cockerel weathervane is now mounted on a short post, rather than a tall flagpole. The medieval flintwork is offset by the mellow brickwork of the 1736 chancel and south chapel, although the lower parts of these walls are also medieval, and the 18th-century porch gives a charming domestic feel to the church.

PENN
Church Road c1955 P283004

At the Church Road junction with Paul's Hill there is a small triangular green with a war memorial cross (out of view to the left) and in 1955 a large and ancient tree, now replaced by a young one. Beyond, to the west, are the churchyard's flint and brick boundary walls. The nearer Victorian building on the right has gone, replaced by housing association dwellings, Penn Mead, in about 1960. Beyond is a former girl's primary school designed by Edward Blore in 1839 and extended (the right-hand gable) in 1910. It is now Holy Trinity's parish office and church hall.

BEACONSFIELD, *Windsor End c1955* B609023

Beaconsfield, another good Chiltern market town, has four streets or 'ends' meeting at these cross-roads, even in the 1950s with a roundabout. Now by-passed by the M40 since the 1970s, the town is quieter. This view was taken looking down Windsor End with the Saracen's Head on the left, designed by the ubiquitous Arthur Vernon in 1895 (see T354006, page 79). The churchyard is on the right; to the right of the 1921 war memorial surmounted by its lantern (right), we can just make out the obelisk marking the poet Edmund Waller's tomb. He built Hall Barn, a mid 17th-century mansion in historic parkland, now cut off from the town by the M40.

BEACONSFIELD
The Roundabout c1965 B609103

This view was taken looking north-east from the war memorial to London End on the right and the start of Aylesbury End on the left by the White Hart. The run of buildings between it and the Saracen's Head on the south side of London End have numerous timber-frames concealed behind 18th- and 19th-century brick facades: some 16th- and 17th-century chimney stacks of old thin bricks are visible above the tiled roofs. As in Amersham, the facades are often deceptive, for in the era of Georgian prosperity most of the surviving timber-framed houses in towns had a more fashionable brick front added.

BEACONSFIELD
Bekonscot Model Village c1965 B609131

Beaconsfield is famous for the model village of Bekonscot, which is in Warwick Road, a turning to the right beyond the Waitrose car park entrance in Beaconsfield New Town north of the railway line. Here in 1929 a local accountant, Roland Callingham, started a scale model village in what was then a field. Now surrounded by 1930s and 1950s houses, Bekonscot is a quaint, charming and popular visitor attraction, with nearly a hundred different buildings. A key feature is this miniature railway, which winds through the 'village'. Note the three-rail electrical system, known to all boys who in the 1950s had Hornby-Dublo model train sets.

▼ **LITTLE MARLOW,** *The Parish Church Interior 1890* 23695

From Beaconsfield the route heads south-west to the River Thames, which from Wooburn forms the south boundary of the Chilterns as far west as Reading. From there it turns north to the Goring Gap; the Chilterns finish at Wallingford, to continue westward as the Berkshire Downs. One of the most attractive near-riverside villages is Little Marlow, with its 17th- and 18th-century manor house beyond 17th-century brick churchyard walls. This view of the interior of St John the Baptist's Parish Church shows the low chancel arch. The oil lamps have been replaced by electric ones since 1890.

▶ **MARLOW**
The Parish Church and the River Thames 1890 27228

Marlow was once a riverside port, like Henley (view 27193, pages 106-107), handling High Wycombe's corn, firewood and timber trade. It is now a fashionable town, and a far cry from the days when wharfingers' cries echoed through the streets. By 1890 it had already changed, for the Thames had become more of a leisure river, as witnessed by the oarsmen pulling away upstream from the lock which by-passes the weir. On the left is Tierney Clark's 1830s suspension bridge. The 1830s parish church of All Saints' still has its knobbly spire; it was replaced in 1899 by the present more delicate one.

◄ **MARLOW**
High Street 1890
23689

The High Street runs north from the Thames; it is flanked by many good Georgian facades, some of which hide earlier timber-framed houses. There has been more change on the right-hand side, with 1970s rebuildings on each side of the shop with two black-painted bay windows. In the distance is the Crown Hotel, now a Boots the chemist; the Crown has taken over the town hall, just out of view to the left. The two left-hand Georgian houses now have railings separating them from the street.

▶ **MARLOW**
The Compleat Angler Hotel c1960 M35048

The Compleat Angler Hotel is nowadays much extended, mostly in neo-Georgian style and the gap between the buildings has closed. Originally the river bridge across the Thames was to the left of the hotel, and its facade fronted this road. When the suspension bridge opened in 1831, a new road to Bisham turned the front into a rear elevation, and the Victorian wings here attempted to address this reversal. This view looks across from All Saints' riverside churchyard.

► **HAMBLEDEN**
Greenlands 1890
27215

Westwards the river passes Medmenham and Hambleden; Greenlands stands a mile west of Hambleden. This was the home of W H Smith, the newsagent, who was ennobled as Lord Hambleden and who subsequently gave the National Trust covenants over most of the Hambleden valley. The house is now Henley Management College, with modern buildings to the north and east of the house. This view captures it before W H Smith's major enlargements in 1894 and 1905, and after the then owner Edward Marjoribanks had added a belvedere tower in 1853 (now gone) and clad the house in Italianate stucco decoration.

◄ **PRINCES RISBOROUGH**
The Parish Church c1955 P282022

The route now leaves the river to head northwards across the Chilterns to its northern flanks, starting in the small market town of Princes Risborough. Granted a market charter by Henry VIII in 1523, it had a royal manor house on a moated site west of the churchyard. Here the Black Prince had a stud farm and deer park, hence the town's name, to distinguish it from nearby Monks Risborough. The moated site is now unromantically represented by the tarmac Mount car park. The parish church has one of Buckinghamshire's few stone spires; but this is a modern one of 1908 by Oldrid Scott, who also built Marlow church's later spire.

▲ **PRINCES RISBOROUGH,** *Church Street c1955* P282018

Church Street leads east from the site of the Black Prince's manor house, the church and the present 17th-century manor house to the Market Square. The early 19th-century market hall behind the camera has a room over an open ground floor and is crowned by a clock turret cupola. The jettied timber-framed 16th-century building on the right was a row of cottages condemned in the 1930s for slum clearance. Saved by a local solicitor, they eventually served as the local branch library from the 1950s until 1986; the building is now a Chinese restaurant.

◄ **PRINCES RISBOROUGH**
High Street c1955 P282008

From Market Square, Frith's photographer looked south-east down the High Street. In the far distance is the former White Lion pub. It was saved in the 1980s from a road improvement scheme that turned Back Lane (behind the buildings on the left) into a relief road; this was admittedly to the benefit of the High Street and the town centre, which was then on the route of the A4010 Aylesbury to High Wycombe road. On the left is the George and Dragon, a former coaching inn.

WHITELEAF
The Cross and the Chilterns
1897 39644

The ancient Icknield Way, a
Neolithic route from East Anglia
to Salisbury Plain, runs between
Princes Risborough and the Chiltern
escarpment. Once out of the Chilterns
at Goring it is known as the Ridgeway.
This early view was taken from the
Icknield Way towards Whiteleaf
Cross, a chalk-cut cross with a large
triangular base that can be seen
from miles away. It is currently
being restored, but its origins are
uncertain - the theories are legion.
There is another one further along the
escarpment at Bledlow. The earliest
known reference to the Whiteleaf
Cross is as late as 1742.

WENDOVER, *Coombe Hill and the Cross Roads c1955* G241022

Continuing north-east along the lower slopes of the Chiltern escarpment, Frith's photographer paused at Butlers Cross crossroads to look towards Coombe Hill and its monument (centre left), a view now obscured by the trees that now fill the gap.
The views from the summit of Coombe Hill at over 850 feet are magnificent, extending for miles over the Vale of Aylesbury.
Owned by the National Trust since 1918, the centrepiece of the hill is the stone Boer War memorial column erected in 1904;
it was destroyed by lightning in 1938 and rebuilt by the County Council, this time with lightning conductors.

WENDOVER
From the South 1901 47477

This rather gloomy view was taken on the track down from Coombe Hill (view G241022 page 86) on Bacombe Hill, heading east towards Wendover in the middle distance, another of the Chilterns' fine small market towns. The photographer was on bare grazed downland, but since then Bacombe Hill has become heavily wooded. The white scar in the middle distance is the line of the then recent Metropolitan Railway from Marylebone to Aylesbury, which opened in 1892. In the distance are Wendover Woods. Within them is the highest point of the Chilterns at 876 feet, and an Iron Age hillfort on Boddington Hill.

WENDOVER, *The Pond 1901* 47475

The last view in this chapter is a restful one; it was taken east of Wendover town centre and near the parish church, which is some way south of the main streets on a rural lane by the former manor house, now a school. The photographer was on Heron Path, a footpath that leads to the town, and beyond the distant trees the old Amersham Road is now a quiet way into town, now that Wendover has at last got its by-pass. The pond is nowadays weed-free; it is a delightful and quiet haven, with footpaths around the pond edge.

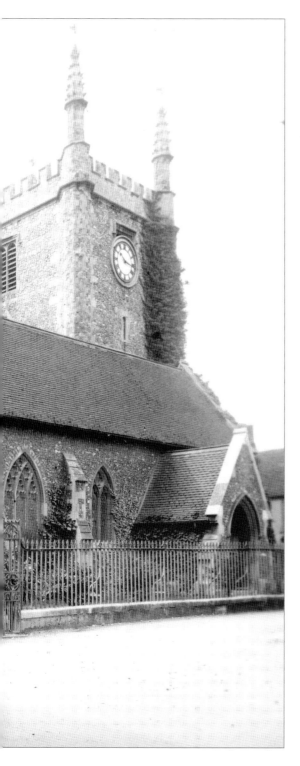

WALLINGFORD AND THE OXFORDSHIRE CHILTERNS

WALLINGFORD, *St Mary's Parish Church 1890* 27028

The last chapter in this book moves west into the Oxfordshire Chilterns. We start at Wallingford on the former Berkshire bank, an Anglo-Saxon burgh founded in the late ninth century to guard a strategic river crossing. It gained its first market charter from Henry II in 1155, and was a prosperous town until Abingdon took much of its trade in the 15th century. At one time it had a dozen parish churches, but now only three remain. St Mary's in the Market Place retains its medieval tower; the rest was rebuilt in 1854. To the right is the corner of the fine Town Hall of 1670.

WALLINGFORD, *St Peter's Church 1899* 42990

The second surviving parish church, St Peter's, in Thames Street, is a medieval foundation, but it was entirely rebuilt in the 1760s and 1770s. It has a most unusual Gothick octagonal bell stage and a tall delicate spire with four storeys of arches. It is a delightful and delicate piece of work by the classicist Sir Robert Taylor, who was working in an unfamiliar style. This view was taken from the Oxfordshire bank. Wallingford's long bridge is out of view to the right, a long one with a causeway across the water meadows, and much rebuilt, but with medieval work surviving.

WALLINGFORD
The Lawns, Castle Priory
c1960 W10099

Wallingford has many fine houses. It is remarkable, too, that much of the Anglo-Saxon ramparts survive, as well as the earthworks and motte of the late 11th-century castle at the north-east corner of the town. There are also some substantial houses in large gardens, and Castle Priory on Thames Street is one. There was a small Benedictine priory in the town in the Middle Ages, but this house has nothing to do with that or the castle. This view is of the river front of the late 18th-century house from the lawns, although the house is largely screened from the river by trees and shrubs.

WALLINGFORD, *St Leonard's Church and Lower Wharf 1893* 31708

Moving further south along the Oxfordshire bank, Frith's Victorian photographer looked across to the tower of the third surviving parish church, St Leonard's. The tower is not genuinely Norman - the church suffered at the hands of Henry Hakewill in 1849 - but the rest of the church is Norman, although Hakewill added the south nave arcade and generally infuriatingly over-restored the church. Corneby's the boat builders' building has recently been rebuilt as a two storey house. The gables and chimneys to the left, behind the wharf, belong to St Lucians, a fine 16th- and 17th-century house.

WALLINGFORD *from the air 1920* AF891

▼ **WALLINGFORD,** *From Winterbrook Ferry 1890* 27026

The last view of Wallingford is also from the Oxfordshire bank, taken on a tranquil day. In the middle distance the tower of St Leonard's Church peeps above the trees, and in the far distance is the river bridge; this is partly medieval but with the central three arches rebuilt in 1809 and flanked by arches rebuilt in 1751. The other twelve arches are to the causeway rather than over the river. Winterbrook is a hamlet immediately south of the town - needless to say, the ferry no longer operates.

► **WALLINGFORD**
Mongewell House 1893 31710

A mile south of Wallingford, Mongewell is on the Oxfordshire bank; Mongewell House and the ruined Norman parish church are all that survive of a deserted medieval village. The present Mongewell House dates from 1891, and replaces a Georgian predecessor. Built in a heavy Wren style, since 1953 it has been part of Carmel College, a Jewish college, conference and residential centre. Many new buildings have been added in the Georgian landscaped park, including a spectacular synagogue of 1963. The Ridgeway long distance footpath passes through the grounds and park.

◄ WALLINGFORD
Shillingford Bridge c1955
W10025

Two miles north of Wallingford, in the lee of river cliffs, the road to Dorchester and Oxford crosses the Thames at Shillingford on an elegant three-arch stone bridge of 1827. This was a toll bridge until 1874, and replaced earlier ones which in their turn had replaced a ferry. I assume the name 'shilling ford' is a coincidence, as that would be a very expensive Tudor fee. To the left is the former Swan Hotel, now the Shillingford Bridge Hotel, a Georgian building much altered and extended.

► EWELME
The Village c1960 E59023

Moving away from the River Thames back into the Chiltern hills, beyond Benson and its huge RAF airfield, the tour reaches the tranquil village of Ewelme, which is set in a narrow valley with a stream flowing by the main street. The stream can be seen on the left of this view, which looks north-west towards the west end of the High Street and Thatchings, the thatched cottage. The house and chapel on the left have been replaced by Suffolk House, built in 1977 'out of the gift of Alice Duchess of Suffolk who founded God's House in Ewelme 1436' - of which more in view E59007, page 98.

EWELME
The Village c1960
E59027

Further south-east in the High Street, the church and almshouses are some hundred yards behind Frith's photographer. The 18th-century Greyhound (left) is no longer a pub, but commemorates the building's past history in renaming itself Greyhound House. Beyond the 1950s bungalow on the right and East Cottage is now a close of 1990s houses, Wingfield Close. In the distance is the thatched village hall.

97

▼ **EWELME,** *The Parish Church and the Almshouses c1955* E59007

The village is set apart by its breathtaking, sumptuous 15th-century church, almshouses and school group founded by the Earl and Countess of Suffolk. The Countess was the granddaughter of the poet Geoffrey Chaucer, and her alabaster effigy is in the church. The Suffolks rebuilt the church in about 1432, and built the school and founded the almshouses, or God's House, both in 1437. The school and almshouses are mostly in brick, which was rare in Oxfordshire at this date. It is a wonderful complex, and the school is still in use after all these centuries as the local primary school. This view shows the almshouses, which surround a central cloister, to the right.

▶ **WATLINGTON**
The Town Hall c1950
W254002

From Ewelme the tour heads north-east to Watlington, a small market town at the foot of the Chilterns and on the Lower Icknield Way. Full of character and interesting buildings, the town has at its centre this brick town hall built in 1665. However, the section on the right, with single-light windows one above the other, was added in the 19th century. It was paid for by Thomas Stonor of Stonor Park, five miles to the south-east. As with most market halls, the ground floor was originally open, and gave shelter to the market stalls.

◄ WATLINGTON
Couching Street c1965 W254035

The photographer is now further south down Couching Street, with the town hall in the distance. This narrow road is the main route through the town towards Thame; it is very much still a bottleneck, with a very narrow pinch point beyond the Town Hall. Two- and three-storey houses, some brick or render, some with exposed timber-framing, line the street. The overbearing rendered gable to Couching House of 1906 in the middle distance on the left seems the only jarring element.

► WATLINGTON
Brook Street c1955
W254022

Brook Street (the B480) is the main street running east to west, with Couching Street (view W254035) a left turn just before the timber-framed cottage in the distance, Pilgrim Cottage. The Black Lion is no longer a pub, while the cottage by the telegraph pole and the walls beyond have long gone, to be replaced by 1970s cottages that turn the corner into Couching Street.

WATLINGTON
Old Cottages, Church Street c1955 W254027

Resistance to the Railway Age, particularly by the Earl of Macclesfield at Shirburn Castle to the north-east of the town, preserved Watlington as something of a backwater. When the railway eventually arrived, it was only a branch line from Princes Risborough, and did not lead to dramatic developments. Nearer the town hall the town's architecture is more urbane; but towards the church, cottages you might expect to see in a village appear, such as these 17th-century thatched and timber-framed ones in Church Street. The left-hand one is named, somewhat obviously, The Thatch.

▶ **WATLINGTON**
The Barley Mow
c1950 W254003

High Street runs west from the town hall crossroads. Here Frith's photographer looked along the street past the 17th-century timber-framed and jettied Barley Mow (left), now a house called The Old Barley Mow and with the render removed to expose the timbers. The rendered building on the right with the wall-mounted streetlight is 18th-century, and now the War Memorial Club. The two shop fronts (right), one the baker's, have been replaced by not nearly as attractive modern shop fronts. In the distance beyond the Hovis sign is the war memorial cross itself and the start of Church Street.

◀ **NETTLEBED**
The Bull Hotel and High Street c1955 N79023

Climbing the Chiltern escarpment southwards, the route then descends steadily to Nettlebed, about five miles to the south. The prosperous Georgian and later houses testify to its wealth, which was based on brick making and its position on the Henley to Oxford turnpiked road. The Bull Hotel (right) was one of the village's two main coaching inns – it is now a house. This view captures well the town-like character of this part of the main street.

▲ **NETTLEBED,** *The White Hart Hotel c1955* N79011

A little west of the Old Bull and on the north side of the main street is the other former coaching inn, the White Hart Hotel, which is still a pub and hotel. It is an early Georgian building in brick and flint; it retains cross-casement windows, rather than having been modernised with sliding sash windows. Admittedly the present ones replace the originals. The cottage to the left, The Myrtles, is now incorporated in the hotel.

◄ **NETTLEBED**
Watlington Street c1955
N79008

Watlington Street, a left turn where the main road reaches the common, is on a very different architectural scale to the Henley-Oxford road of the previous two views. Here the scene is more cottage-like and less urban before giving way to modern housing along the road to Watlington. The K6 telephone kiosk remains (its paintwork is now in better condition), and the post office building has been altered, but it is still 'Nettlebed Village Shop and Sub Post Office'. The Sun Inn is now Mozarts, an Austrian bar and restaurant.

▼ **NETTLEBED,** *Joyce Grove c1955* N79014

The grounds of Joyce Grove are entered via ornate gates opposite the Watlington Road and Henley Road junction, and the public are welcome to stroll in the grounds. This somewhat grandiose Jacobethan mansion was built in 1904, using red brick and copious amounts of Bath stone. Long a nursing home (note the nurse in an upstairs window, left) it is now a Sue Ryder Home, and virtually unchanged. Its grounds are splendid, and the mansion has a claim to fame: it was the boyhood home of Ian Fleming, creator of James Bond.

▶ **NETTLEBED**
The Woods c1955 N79018

North-east and south-east of Nettlebed there are extensive wooded commons, large areas of them pock-marked with old pits, now grown over. These were clay pits used for extracting the raw material for Nettlebed's former major industry. It was an important brick and tile making centre from the 14th century onwards; for example, it supplied 35,000 bricks for Wallingford Castle in 1365, and others for Stonor chapel tower in 1416. There is a preserved bottle kiln just east of the Watlington Street junction amid the houses of a modern close. This was built in the 18th century, and was last used in 1938.

◄ **HENLEY-ON-THAMES**
Market Place 1893
31732

Continuing along the A4130, the tour reaches Henley and is back on the River Thames. This historic view of the market place from Hart Street shows the old town hall of 1795 with its pedimented two-storey portico. This was replaced by the present Town Hall in 1899-1901, while the ornate Gothic drinking fountain, an 1885 memorial to a vicar, had a short sojourn here, being moved in 1903 to a site near St Mary's church. At the right is the entry to Bell Street. Thackara's (left), now a menswear shop, is on the corner of Duke Street.

▶ **HENLEY-ON-THAMES**
Hart Street and St Mary's Church c1955 H73007

This view was taken from Henley's fine Georgian river bridge, completed in 1786 and replacing a series of earlier bridges that go back to about 1170. The view shows Hart Street, with one of the timber-framed houses on the left noted as the birthplace of William Lenthall in 1591. He was Speaker of the Long Parliament during the Civil War. To the right is St Mary's Church; the earliest reference to it is from 1204, but the existing building is mostly 14th- and 15th-century. The west tower was built between 1521 and 1547, while the chapel behind the steps dates from 1789.

HENLEY-ON-THAMES
The Riverside 1890
27193

Henley was an important market town and a key river port; corn and timber were its chief exports until well into the 19th century. This view shows the town still with its old trades (there is a timber wharf to the right) but also in its new guise as a riverside leisure town famed for its Regatta. For beside the rowing skiff, the frontage of the timber yard has a temporary grandstand, and the many gabled boathouses have viewing balconies for the regatta (see view 27204 pages 108-109). Behind these are the chimneys and brew tower of Brakspear's brewery, which closed in 2003.

▶ **HENLEY-ON-THAMES**
The Regatta 1890 27204

Henley had been the venue for the very first Oxford and Cambridge Boat Race in 1829, and in 1839 the first Regatta was held. It became an annual fixture, a key event in the English social calendar, and vital to the town's economy after the loss of the coaching and river commerce to the new railways. This view looks northwards from the south bank past the grounds of Phyllis Court and Fawley House during the 1890 Regatta, with many watching from houseboats moored along the banks. Many of these were more like floating hotels with viewing galleries above.

◄ HENLEY-ON-THAMES
The Landing Stage and the Steamer 'Goring'
c1955 H73025

Henley is now sleek, prosperous and middle class; as with Marlow, it is difficult to imagine its streets loud with bargees and watermen's cries and the river bank wharves piled high with grain and timber. Nowadays, and indeed for most of the 20th century, messing about on boats and strolling along the river bank has been the main activity of these former wharves. Hobbs & Sons (right) is one of the oldest boatbuilder's and yards in the town, and still thrives today. In this view, Salters Steamers' steamer, 'Goring', is arriving back from a river cruise with an eager queue awaiting the next trip.

HENLEY-ON-THAMES
Marsh Lock c1955
H73050

Marsh, a mile upstream from Henley and on the Berkshire bank, was where much of the corn from the Chiltern fields was ground into flour for Henley's trade; it was brought from Marsh Mill, a huge watermill, to the town by wagons. The mill buildings have long gone, along with Henley's corn trade, and the lock is now used almost exclusively by leisure craft by-passing the weir seen on the right of this view. Here a steam launch enters the lock, supervised by the peak-capped lock-keeper.

▼ **GORING,** *From Streatley Hills 1896* 38305

The chalk hills are cut through by the River Thames, the Chilterns on the Oxfordshire side and the Berkshire Downs to the west. From Neolithic times onwards the river has been crossed at Goring. Oxfordshire's Icknield Way becomes the Ridgeway on the Berkshire or Streatley side. This view looks across to Goring on the right with the Thames and the river bridge that replaced the ancient ferry. The parish church can also be seen; it is surprising that Brunel's Great Western Railway cannot. The village has grown a lot, with riverside villas combining with commuter housing to ring its historic core.

▶ **GORING**
The Parish Church 1890 27039

The heart of the old village is a little east of the river, on higher and drier land, with the church nearest the river. St Thomas of Canterbury's Parish Church is mostly Norman, although the tower battlements and upper windows and the chapel are later medieval. The semi-circular apse looks very 12th-century indeed, but it actually dates from 1887, replacing the original. This had been demolished in the late 12th century when a small Augustinian priory was founded here; its church was attached to the east end of the parish church, minus its apse. The nuns, the priory buildings and their church have all long disappeared.

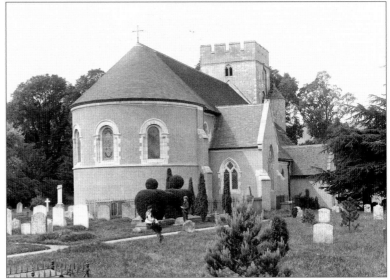

◄ **GORING**
The Miller of Mansfield Hotel 1900 45469

North-east of the church, at the junction of Manor Road and High Street, the Miller of Mansfield is a well known hotel, viewed here in 1900 when the right-hand gabled wing and the chimneystack had recently been completed. The left-hand part with the two bay windows flanking the porch is Georgian, while the block to the right was a later 19th-century cottage taken over by the hotel - its porch door was blocked and turned into a window. This is nowadays a porch again, but the rustic timber fencing has long gone.

► **GORING**
Manor Road 1904
52927

Heading south along Manor Road, Frith's Edwardian photographer looked north, with Ferry Lane just to the left out of view. The butcher's shop is now Norfolk House and a marketing consultancy offices, but Tudor Cottage beyond survives, apart from the timber-framed gabled bay which has been rebuilt recently. On the right is the John Barleycorn pub, now somewhat smartened up, while the big house behind the tall tree is now The Old Vicarage.

GORING
The Lock c1955 G34006

Goring Lock by-passes the weir across the Thames. This view looks upstream, with a small river cruiser, 'Galeka', entering the lock, which was entirely reconstructed in 1922. The lock keeper's cottage on the left was rebuilt in the 1880s and is now, somewhat regrettably, painted white. In recent years the lock has been lengthened to take larger boats. Concealed by the horse chestnuts are some prosperous riverside villas dating from Goring's expansion around 1900.

GORING
The Boathouses c1955
G34024

To the right of the lock island is a creek terminating at the foot of the bridge. In 1838 the bridge had replaced the ferry which ran from the river end of Ferry Lane some two hundreds yards to the south of the present bridge. The bridge is behind the photographer. A thatched riverside house stands beyond Edwardian boathouses, in the 1950s owned by Hobbs & Sons of Henley (see view H73025, pages 110-111), to the right. The much gabled upper floor is now The Boathouse Surgery, and the street front, in effect at first floor level, is now a post office.

GORING, *The Heath c1955* G34032

This chapter concludes some five miles south-east of Goring itself back up on the Chiltern plateau, here well wooded. The former post office is at a crossroads east of the featureless hamlet of Goring Heath. It stands some three hundred yards south of the fine almshouses founded in 1724 by Henry Alnutt, a former Lord Mayor of London, an unexpected sight out in the countryside. Straight ahead leads to Mapledurham and Reading, and the road on which Frith's photographer stood leads to Cary's Pond and back to Goring. Barrett's General Stores and Post Office date from around 1900.

INDEX

The Francis Frith Collection Titles

www.francisfrith.com

The Francis Frith Collection publishes over 100 new titles each year. A selection of those currently available is listed below. For latest catalogue please contact The Francis Frith Collection.
Town Books 96 pages, approximately 75 photos. **County and Themed Books** 128 pages, approximately 135 photos (unless specified). Pocket Albums are miniature editions of Frith local history books 128 pages, approximately 95 photos.

Accrington Old and New
Alderley Edge and Wilmslow
Amersham, Chesham and Rickmansworth
Andover
Around Abergavenny
Around Alton
Aylesbury
Barnstaple
Bedford
Bedfordshire
Berkshire Living Memories
Berkshire Pocket Album
Blackpool Pocket Album
Bognor Regis
Bournemouth
Bradford
Bridgend
Bridport
Brighton and Hove
Bristol
Buckinghamshire
Calne Living Memories
Camberley Pocket Album
Canterbury Cathedral
Cardiff Old and New
Chatham and the Medway Towns
Chelmsford
Chepstow Then and Now
Cheshire
Cheshire Living Memories
Chester
Chesterfield
Chigwell
Christchurch
Churches of East Cornwall
Clevedon
Clitheroe
Corby Living Memories
Cornish Coast
Cornwall Living Memories
Cotswold Living Memories
Cotswold Pocket Album
Coulsdon, Chipstead and Woodmanstern
County Durham
Cromer, Sheringham and Holt
Dartmoor Pocket Album
Derby
Derbyshire
Derbyshire Living Memories
Devon
Devon Churches
Dorchester

Dorset Coast Pocket Album
Dorset Living Memories
Dorset Villages
Down the Dart
Down the Severn
Down the Thames
Dunmow, Thaxted and Finchingfield
Durham
East Anglia Pocket Album
East Devon
East Grinstead
Edinburgh
Ely and The Fens
Essex Pocket Album
Essex Second Selection
Essex: The London Boroughs
Exeter
Exmoor
Falmouth
Farnborough, Fleet and Aldershot
Folkestone
Frome
Furness and Cartmel Peninsulas
Glamorgan
Glasgow
Glastonbury
Gloucester
Gloucestershire
Greater Manchester
Guildford
Hailsham
Hampshire
Harrogate
Hastings and Bexhill
Haywards Heath Living Memories
Heads of the Valleys
Heart of Lancashire Pocket Album
Helston
Herefordshire
Horsham
Humberside Pocket Album
Huntingdon, St Neots and St Ives
Hythe, Romney Marsh and Ashford
Ilfracombe
Ipswich Pocket Album
Isle of Wight
Isle of Wight Living Memories
King's Lynn
Kingston upon Thames
Lake District Pocket Album
Lancashire Living Memories
Lancashire Villages

Available from your local bookshop or from the publisher

The Francis Frith Collection Titles (continued)

Lancaster, Morecambe and Heysham Pocket Album
Leeds Pocket Album
Leicester
Leicestershire
Lincolnshire Living Memoires
Lincolnshire Pocket Album
Liverpool and Merseyside
London Pocket Album
Ludlow
Maidenhead
Maidstone
Malmesbury
Manchester Pocket Album
Marlborough
Matlock
Merseyside Living Memories
Nantwich and Crewe
New Forest
Newbury Living Memories
Newquay to St Ives
North Devon Living Memories
North London
North Wales
North Yorkshire
Northamptonshire
Northumberland
Northwich
Nottingham
Nottinghamshire Pocket Album
Oakham
Odiham Then and Now
Oxford Pocket Album
Oxfordshire
Padstow
Pembrokeshire
Penzance
Petersfield Then and Now
Plymouth
Poole and Sandbanks
Preston Pocket Album
Ramsgate Old and New
Reading Pocket Album
Redditch Living Memories
Redhill to Reigate
Richmond
Ringwood
Rochdale
Romford Pocket Album
Salisbury Pocket Album
Scotland
Scottish Castles
Sevenoaks and Tonbridge
Sheffield and South Yorkshire Pocket Album
Shropshire
Somerset
South Devon Coast
South Devon Living Memories
South East London

Southampton Pocket Album
Southend Pocket Album
Southport
Southwold to Aldeburgh
Stourbridge Living Memories
Stratford upon Avon
Stroud
Suffolk
Suffolk Pocket Album
Surrey Living Memories
Sussex
Sutton
Swanage and Purbeck
Swansea Pocket Album
Swindon Living Memories
Taunton
Teignmouth
Tenby and Saundersfoot
Tiverton
Torbay
Truro
Uppingham
Villages of Kent
Villages of Surrey
Villages of Sussex Pocket Album
Wakefield and the Five Towns Living Memories
Warrington
Warwick
Warwickshire Pocket Album
Wellingborough Living Memories
Wells
Welsh Castles
West Midlands Pocket Album
West Wiltshire Towns
West Yorkshire
Weston-super-Mare
Weymouth
Widnes and Runcorn
Wiltshire Churches
Wiltshire Living Memories
Wiltshire Pocket Album
Wimborne
Winchester Pocket Album
Windermere
Windsor
Wirral
Wokingham and Bracknell
Woodbridge
Worcester
Worcestershire
Worcestershire Living Memories
Wyre Forest
York Pocket Album
Yorkshire
Yorkshire Coastal Memories
Yorkshire Dales
Yorkshire Revisited

See Frith books on the internet at www.francisfrith.com

FRITH PRODUCTS & SERVICES

Francis Frith would doubtless be pleased to know that the pioneering publishing venture he started in 1860 still continues today. Over a hundred and forty years later, The Francis Frith Collection continues in the same innovative tradition and is now one of the foremost publishers of vintage photographs in the world. Some of the current activities include:

INTERIOR DECORATION

Today Frith's photographs can be seen framed and as giant wall murals in thousands of pubs, restaurants, hotels, banks, retail stores and other public buildings throughout the country. In every case they enhance the unique local atmosphere of the places they depict and provide reminders of gentler days in an increasingly busy and frenetic world.

PRODUCT PROMOTIONS

Frith products are used by many major companies to promote the sales of their own products or to reinforce their own history and heritage. Frith promotions have been used by Hovis bread, Courage beers, Scots Porage Oats, Colman's mustard, Cadbury's foods, Mellow Birds coffee, Dunhill pipe tobacco, Guinness, and Bulmer's Cider.

GENEALOGY AND FAMILY HISTORY

As the interest in family history and roots grows world-wide, more and more people are turning to Frith's photographs of Great Britain for images of the towns, villages and streets where their ancestors lived; and, of course, photographs of the churches and chapels where their ancestors were christened, married and buried are an essential part of every genealogy tree and family album.

FRITH PRODUCTS

All Frith photographs are available Framed or just as Mounted Prints and Posters (size 23 x 16 inches). These may be ordered from the address below. Other products available are- Address Books, Calendars, Jigsaws, Canvas Prints, Notelets and local and prestige books.

THE INTERNET

Already ninety thousand Frith photographs can be viewed and purchased on the internet through the Frith websites and a myriad of partner sites.

For more detailed information on Frith companies and products, look at this site:
www.francisfrith.com

See the complete list of Frith Books at: www.francisfrith.com
This web site is regularly updated with the latest list of publications from The Francis Frith Collection. If you wish to buy books relating to another part of the country that your local bookshop does not stock, you may purchase on-line.

For further information, trade, or author enquiries please contact us at the address below:
The Francis Frith Collection, Unit 6, Oakley Business Park, Wylye Road, Dinton, Wiltshire SP3 5EU.
Tel: +44 (0)1722 716 376 Fax: +44 (0)1722 716 881 Email: sales@francisfrith.co.uk

---

See Frith products on the internet at www.francisfrith.com

FREE PRINT OF YOUR CHOICE

Mounted Print
Overall size 14 x 11 inches (355 x 280mm)

Choose any Frith photograph in this book.
Simply complete the Voucher opposite and return it with your remittance for £3.50 (to cover postage and handling) and we will print the photograph of your choice in SEPIA (size 11 x 8 inches) and supply it in a cream mount with a burgundy rule line (overall size 14 x 11 inches).
Please note: aerial photographs and photographs with a reference number starting with a "Z" are not Frith photographs and cannot be supplied under this offer. Offer valid for delivery to one UK address only.

PLUS: **Order additional Mounted Prints at HALF PRICE - £9.50 each** (normally £19.00)
If you would like to order more Frith prints from this book, possibly as gifts for friends and family, you can buy them at half price (with no additional postage and handling costs).

PLUS: **Have your Mounted Prints framed**
For an extra £18.00 per print you can have your mounted print(s) framed in an elegant polished wood and gilt moulding, overall size 16 x 13 inches (no additional postage and handling required).

IMPORTANT!

These special prices are only available if you use this form to order. You must use the ORIGINAL VOUCHER on this page (no copies permitted). We can only despatch to one UK address. This offer cannot be combined with any other offer.

Send completed Voucher form to:
The Francis Frith Collection, Unit 6, Oakley Business Park, Wylye Road, Dinton, Wiltshire SP3 5EU

CHOOSE A PHOTOGRAPH FROM THIS BOOK

Voucher for **FREE** and Reduced Price Frith Prints

Please do not photocopy this voucher. Only the original is valid, so please fill it in, cut it out and return it to us with your order.

Picture ref no	Page no	Qty	Mounted @ £9.50	Framed + £18.00	Total Cost £
		1	Free of charge*	£	£
			£9.50	£	£
			£9.50	£	£
			£9.50	£	£
			£9.50	£	£
			£9.50	£	£
Please allow 28 days for delivery. Offer available to one UK address only			* Post & handling		£3.50
			Total Order Cost		£

Title of this book . . . .

I enclose a cheque/postal order for £ . . . .
made payable to 'The Francis Frith Collection'

OR please debit my Mastercard / Visa / Maestro card, details below

Card Number:

Issue No (Maestro only):   Valid from (Maestro):

Card Security Number: Expires:

Signature:

Name Mr/Mrs/Ms . . . .

Address . . . .

. . . .

. . . .

. . . . Postcode . . . .

Daytime Tel No . . . .

Email . . . .

978-1-84589-557-0   Valid to 31/12/12

Can you help us with information about any of the Frith photographs in this book?

We are gradually compiling an historical record for each of the photographs in the Frith archive. It is always fascinating to find out the names of the people shown in the pictures, as well as insights into the shops, buildings and other features depicted.

If you recognize anyone in the photographs in this book, or if you have information not already included in the author's caption, do let us know. We would love to hear from you, and will try to publish it in future books or articles.

An Invitation from The Francis Frith Collection to Share Your Memories

The 'Share Your Memories' feature of our website allows members of the public to add personal memories relating to the places featured in our photographs, or comment on others already added. Seeing a place from your past can rekindle forgotten or long held memories. Why not visit the website, find photographs of places you know well and add YOUR story for others to read and enjoy? We would love to hear from you!

www.francisfrith.com/memories

Our production team

Frith books are produced by a small dedicated team at offices near Salisbury. Most have worked with the Frith Collection for many years. All have in common one quality: they have a passion for the Frith Collection.

Frith Books and Gifts

We have a wide range of books and gifts available on our website utilising our photographic archive, many of which can be individually personalised.

www.francisfrith.com